WOMEN IN THE
WORLD ECONOMY

WOMEN IN THE WORLD ECONOMY

An INSTRAW Study

United Nations
International Research and Training
Institute for the Advancement of Women

PREPARED BY

Susan P. Joekes

OXFORD UNIVERSITY PRESS
New York   Oxford

Oxford University Press

Oxford   New York   Toronto
Delhi   Bombay   Calcutta   Madras   Karachi
Petaling Jaya   Singapore   Hong Kong   Tokyo
Nairobi   Dar es Salaam   Cape Town
Melbourne   Auckland

and associated companies in
Berlin   Ibadan

Copyright © 1987 by INSTRAW—United Nations

First published in 1987 by Oxford University Press, Inc.,
200 Madison Avenue, New York, New York 10016

First issued as an Oxford University Press paperback, 1989

Oxford is a registered trademark of Oxford University Press

Library of Congress Cataloging-in-Publication data
Joekes, Susan P.
Women in the world economy.

Bibliography: p.
Includes index.
1. Women—Economic conditions—Cross-cultural studies.
2. International economic relations—Cross-cultural
studies. 3. Women—Employment—Cross-cultural studies.
I. International Research and Training Institute for
the Advancement of Women. II. Title.
HQ1381.J64   1987   305.4'3   86-21653
ISBN 0-19-504947-0
ISBN 0-19-506315-5 (pbk)

4   6   8   10   9   7   5   3
Printed in the United States of America

Foreword

Major studies prepared under the auspices of the United Nations represent the work of many minds in a process inherent to the very nature of the Organization. In 1983, the Board of Trustees of INSTRAW decided that the Institute should prepare a series of studies on the role of women in international economic relations, concentrating particularly on an analysis "of the interlinkages between the macro- and micro-levels of the economy and their impact on the role and position of women." That the program of INSTRAW should have such a focus was subsequently affirmed by the United Nations General Assembly in its resolutions 38/104 and 39/122.

Taking different approaches, individual scholars and research institutes specializing in international development questions wrote research papers on trade, money and finance, technology, industry, and agriculture. These technical studies were reviewed at a consultative meeting in Santo Domingo in September 1984, during which an annotated outline for the final study was prepared.* The technical studies were published by INSTRAW in a series entitled *The Role of Women in International Economic Relations*. The Institute is pleased to recognize the contribution of the following authors and institutions for their studies in the series: Rina Berio, Deborah Fahy Bryceson, Sushila Gidwani, Ivan Molina, Achola Pala Okeyo, Amartya K. Sen, Brigitte Stern, North-South Institute, Ottawa, and UNCTAD.

*See the *Report of the Consultative Meeting on the Role of Women in International Economic Relations* (INSTRAW Board of Trustees, 1985, CRP. 1).

v

While the present work is based upon the technical papers, it goes considerably beyond them in its scope and analysis. Moreover, the study reaches a number of findings and makes several policy recommendations. These could have far-reaching policy implications for governments, industrial corporations and financial institutions in both the public and private sectors, nongovernmental and women's organizations, and national and international bodies. As the World Conference to Review and Appraise the Achievements of the United Nations Decade for Women: Equality, Development and Peace adopted the"Nairobi Forward-Looking Strategies," account needs to be taken of the many decisions and proposals on women and international economic relations.

The subject of women and international economic relations is new in the sense that the interlinkages between the two have not yet been adequately analyzed. This study is a first step in that direction. For this reason the study could not take into consideration relevant international decisions and national research findings. It has attempted to steer clear of differing schools of thought choosing the restrictive approach of traditional economic analysis.

The INSTRAW Board of Trustees at its fifth session in January 1985 endorsed the preparation of a comprehensive, consolidated study based on the technical research papers. Under the supervision of the Director of INSTRAW, and with the assistance of Ifigenia Martínez, Philippe de Seynes, Hans W. Singer, Nobuko Takahashi, and Ralph Townley, the study was written by Susan P. Joekes of the Institute of Development Studies at the University of Sussex, England.

Prior to the publication of this study, a high-level group of eminent experts convened 1–3 October 1985 at the Palais des Nations, Geneva, to consider the final draft from the point of view of the changing international economic environment. The Group was invited to give special attention to the need to reassess current economic and social policies and their impact on the position of women in society. At the conclusion of their deliberations, the Group adopted the Statement that follows.

Santo Domingo
March 1986

Dunja Pastizzi-Ferencic, Director
International Research and Training
Institute for the Advancement of Women

Statement Adopted by the Consultative High-Level Expert Meeting on the Role of Women in International Economic Relations

We welcome the invitation by INSTRAW to review and comment on the study *Women in the World Economy* while it is still at a formative stage. In itself, the study represents a significant departure as it examines, in a wealth of detail, the position of women in the world economy, as well as in their countries, communities, and households, and the interrelationship between these contexts. Such a critical study is in response to the INSTRAW Board of Trustees' call for an analysis "of the interlinkages between the macro- and microlevels of the economy and their impact on the role and position of women."

In response to a decision of the Board of Trustees, we were convened by the Director of INSTRAW on 1–3 October 1985 at the Palais des Nations, Geneva. We elected Ambassador Ifigenia Martínez of Mexico as our Moderator. She had been closely associated with the preparation and review of the INSTRAW technical papers which provided much of the material for the present study. We also elected Mrs. Nobuko Takahashi of Japan as our Rapporteur. These, together with the staff and Director of INSTRAW, and the Secretary of the Group, were invited to review the final manuscript before publication. Under such arrangements we found that our discussions were both harmonious and constructive.

We commend the initiative of INSTRAW to review long-term economic development trends, the interlinkages that exist at different levels, and their bearing on women in any of the several economic roles they have acquired or are expected to fulfill. Indeed, the study follows a new road to further innovation that calls for multidisciplinary and cross-cultural approaches. It is our wish that INSTRAW should maintain its initiative in these matters. Such work should keep under continuing review world economic trends and their relationship to women. The assessment of old, and the elaboration of new, policies and strategies of development, whether national or international, should always reflect the findings of such reviews.

The world economic crisis, unprecedented in its duration and extent, serves as the background to this study. The world economy is in disarray and presents profound and at times seemingly intractable problems for many countries and the international community. While markets have become increasingly internationalized, the asymmetries in international economic relations in many ways militate against development. Many developing countries are confronted with a heavy burden of external debt, but at the same time, the means by which this burden can be shouldered are sharply constrained. So severe is the situation that the principles and very texture of international solidarity, which have been so patiently built up, have become increasingly frail. The international mechanisms established to back up world trade, capital flows, and monetary stability have shown themselves to be quite inadequate. While we recognize that perceptions of reality vary, there can be little doubt that the resultant social and economic hardships being faced in developing countries are sufficiently profound to bring impoverishment and dislocation to the lives of many.

The crisis should lead us to reconsider the processes of economic development in all their social and cultural dimensions, as well as the processes of capital formation and increasing productivity. Both the actual and potential dynamic contribution of women in economic activities should be fostered.

We have reviewed and commented on the form and content of the study. While each of us might wish to alter some chapters, introduce additional ideas, or make shifts in emphases, we wish to place on record our support for this stimulating and innovative study, which we see as a pioneering effort to be continued. To provoke professional and action-oriented discussion, the study deserves wide dissemination.

Maria Augusztinovics (Hungary), Mohammed Bedjaoui (Algeria), Herta Daubler Gmelin (Federal Republic of Germany), Ingrid Eide

(Norway), Devaki Jain (India), Ifigenia Martínez (Mexico), Gertrude I. Mongella (Tanzania), Maria Pintasiglio (Portugal), Raul Prebisch (Argentina), Philippe de Seynes (France), Nobuko Takahashi (Japan), and Vida Tomsic (Yugoslavia); Marc Nerfin (International Foundation for Development Alternatives), Krishna Ahooja-Patel (International Labour Organization), Nasha Benabbes-Taarji (United Nations Conference on Trade and Development), Enrique Oteiza (United Nations Research Institute for Social Development).

Palais des Nations, Geneva
3 October 1985

Contents

Part I

WOMEN AND WORLD ECONOMIC ACTIVITY

Part I

WOMEN AND WORLD ECONOMIC ACTIVITY

1

Introduction

The emphasis in studies of women in society has shifted in the past forty years. Early writings revolved around women's traditional roles and centered on their position in the family in "primitive" societies. Anthropologists hailing from other countries produced descriptions of kinship, marriage, and local customs in small communities and examined women's lives in those settings. Men's and women's roles were considered essentially complementary. Narrow in focus as they were, such works were not intended to investigate the broader social and economic milieu nor even to consider economic aspects of different types of social organization.

During the 1970s, the academic literature moved away from studying women in the family toward examining their activities outside the domestic setting and investigating their place in social and economic relations. The idea of a hierarchy in gender relations, of a systematic subordination of women, began to be accepted. The United Nations and other international organizations with humanitarian concerns focused on the relative status of the two sexes in law and social custom and on the need for women to be treated equitably with men. International agreements and national legislation were the recommended approach to improve women's situation.

3

Meanwhile, the women's movement in many societies gathered strength. Studies in developed countries mainly focused on the need to assert women's rights, while in developing countries they attempted to consider women's position within a cross-cultural perspective, often linked to broader topics such as decolonization, class struggle, and ethnicity. Insisting that "the personal is political," the women's movement also prompted the study of interpersonal relations within the family. Lately, it has established the concept of the household as a place where oppression is no less manifest than elsewhere—that is, a microcosm of society, not a haven from its oppressive relations. The household is characterized by conflict among individuals at the same time as its existence is predicated on the gains they make from cooperating with one another.

The study of women in development emerged from these beginnings and has always taken a multidisciplinary approach. Economic growth was at first assumed to be the precursor of social, political, and cultural change bringing improvements to women. Women's position was evaluated with respect to educational and employment opportunity, health status, technological innovation, and institutional representation. Initially, there was more interest in rural than in urban issues. Perhaps as a continuation of the earlier anthropological tradition, much attention was paid to "community development" as an ideal.

Despite the multidisciplinary approach, concern with economic behavior, specifically with work roles, has always been central to the study of women in development. Two approaches have been followed. The first approach categorizes members of the adult population as either "formally employed" or "unemployed," that is, as either gainfully employed or seeking employment. The term *gainful* here covers all work that generates a money income directly or indirectly (so that workers in family enterprises, for example, who may not receive a wage but contribute their labor to an income-generating activity are included). But many activities, particularly in the "informal" sector, were neglected because of the practical difficulties of collecting information about them. Women tend to be concentrated in activities of this kind, so they were omitted from the statistical record more often than men. The invisibility of women's work thus became a common complaint among some economists and policy makers.

The other type of study of employment was not originated by economists. It consisted of examining people's "time budget allocations," observing in minute detail how people spent their days and what kinds of tasks used up their time and energy. Here a very different picture of women's work emerged. Women were shown universally to be working longer hours than men across a spectrum of interrelated tasks that could not be sensibly divided into the conventional economic categories of "productive" and "nonproductive." In this perspective, work on household tasks was understood to be no less onerous or crucial to people's well-being than work outside the home—and individual well-being is, after all, the essence of development. Women's role as primary providers of basic needs thus came to be better appreciated. But there was still a view of women as beneficiaries of development rather than as participants. They were seen, for example, as end-of-the-line dispensers of food and good health, rather than as managers of household resources in an active way.

These two types of approach were never synthesized methodologically. Thus, while it was recognized that women had a heavy work load, the concepts of productive and gainful work, and by extension the term *labor force* itself, did not include this work in economic usage. Since development planners relied on economic terminology in their efforts to promote economic growth, women as a category continued to be left out of account except in "social" or welfare spheres.

In these circumstances, the idea of women as passive beneficiaries of development was soon transformed into the idea of them as victims of change. Development policies, programs, and projects were often criticized for weakening women's position even more by what amounted to neglect on the part of the planners. Development aid, whatever its source, could be seen as delivering resources into the hands of the local or national ruling elite, which tended to overlook women's economic inferiority.

On the analytical side, there was a twofold response to the pessimism inherent in characterizing women as victims. First, the vital interconnection between women's productive work and reproductive work was reaffirmed despite the impossibility of treating them commensurately in economic terms. By extension neither kind of work was supreme; taken together they constituted a double burden. Second, the connotation of passivity that went with the term *victim* was rejected. Women were instead shown to be active and sometimes demanding managers of the only resources at their command, which were usually their own and perhaps their children's labor. But women were always represented within the constraints laid down by prevalent concepts of their gender role. Changes in women's lives resulted from changes in the economic environment and the responses made within that framework, which could still be evaluated as better or worse in terms of the total demands on women's labor time, their nutritional status, their command over money income, and so on. Furthermore, many shifts in economic activity could be understood as resulting from the interaction between the way women spent their time and money and the changes in economic variables as conventionally defined to include prices, consumption patterns, and production techniques. Women ceased to be simple bystanders to the economic action in this perspective. Their actions and decisions were not purely shaped by events in the economic sphere but—bounded always by social relations of gender—played a part in shaping the evolution of economic life.

Attitudes toward the women question in the documents, declarations, and conferences of the United Nations system reflected these changing views of women's first role. Equal rights of men and women are referred to in the United Nations Charter, but the first explicit reference to women and development had to wait until 1970. The General Assembly in that year adopted the Second International Development Decade document, which stated that "the full integration of women in the total development effort should be encouraged." The guiding document for the Third United Nations Development Decade (1980), the *International Development Strategy,* makes frequent references to the desirability of women being involved in the development process. Excerpts from this document are presented in the Annex to this book.

The World Conference of the International Women's Year held in 1975 in Mexico City linked, for the first time, the role of women on a global scale to current and pressing political, social, and development issues. A varied set of world conferences on other topics devoted increasing attention to women's roles along with their primary theme. These conferences included the United Nations Conference on Human Settlements (1976), the Tripartite World Conference on Employment, Income Distribution and Social Progress, and the International Division of Labour (ILO 1976); the United Nations Conference on Desertification (1977), the World Conference on Agrarian Reform and Rural Development (United Nations 1979); and the United Nations Conference on New and Renewable Sources of Energy (1981a). The new, comprehensive, and global approach was confirmed in 1980 at the World Conference of the United Nations Decade for Women at Copenhagen and consolidated in 1985 at the Nairobi Conference to mark the end of the decade.

The data for a global analysis on women's position are limited. Nevertheless, as part of the innovative concepts and approaches generated by the Decade for Women, the International Research and Training Institute for the Advancement of Women (INSTRAW), itself a creation of the Decade, participated in exploring the complexity of issues linking global economic trends with the changing position of women in the economy. The present study is the fruit of this endeavor. It is based to a considerable extent on the series of technical papers published in 1985–86 as part of INSTRAW's research activities. Together, these works reflect the new perspectives opened up by the United Nations Decade for Women. The present study, which was already at a formative stage at the time of the Nairobi Conference (July 1985), may be seen as reinforcing, and being reinforced by, the "Nairobi Forward-Looking Strategies" adopted there. The very lack of consensus on those recommendations of the Conference (United Nations 1985a, paragraphs 98 and 100) dealing with women and international economic relations points up the need for further contributions in this area and underlines the rationale for *Women in the World Economy*.

By the time of the Nairobi Conference marking the end of the Decade in 1985, any suggestion that women are the mere beneficiaries (or victims) of development was firmly set aside; women were now seen as participants and agents of the process. All members of society stand to benefit from a process of development that incorporates women in those capacities. The success of oral rehydration therapy in reducing child mortality in many countries is an example: it is a program that passes control and administration of a vital procedure to women themselves.

Women's systematically disadvantaged economic and social position qualifies them for special consideration. But support is due to them in *all* projects and programs, not just in a separate category of women-only projects. Women's domestic role in rearing children and managing household resources is considered to be of central value to society. The economic importance of the informal sector and of women's labor and enterprise therein are also acknowledged, despite these activities often falling into a gray middle ground between the extremes of formal, fully recorded production on the one hand and the household sphere on the other.

The Decade had three themes: equality, development, and peace. Under equality, the Nairobi Conference recorded the formal gains in women's legal and, to a much lesser extent, political position around the world during the previous ten years. The changes were not insignificant, but they were far less than had been hoped for at the beginning of the Decade. On the peace plane, the picture was more complex. Concern for peace had led to an enormous mobilization of women and men in developed countries protesting the level of violence and of armaments worldwide and the direction of military matters by those whose inclinations were belligerent rather than peaceful. But all the activity, including that of women, apparently did nothing to dampen the rise in military expenditures or the upward escalation of the arms race, even into space. Nor did it seem possible to broaden the acceptance of the concept of the pacific settlement of disputes. Expenditure on armaments diverts labor and capital from productive activity, fuels inflation, and creates asymmetries in the economy that are hard to correct. Finally, 1985 was not a year that was conducive to economic development. When the Nairobi Conference was held, the world was in the deepest and most prolonged recession since the 1930s, which was affecting the world economy in many ways. Some developing countries were ravaged by famine, drought, and ecological collapse, but many more were affected by economic disaster. In many countries, especially in Latin America and Africa, national and personal incomes had fallen twenty to thirty percent in real terms over the previous few years.

International economic factors were predominantly responsible for the depressed state of the world economy. Prices of developing countries' imports and exports and the value of their currencies had fluctuated unpredictably in the 1970s, while countries had become more vulnerable to such instability with their participation in the expansion of international trade and payments since the Second World War. Countries whose terms of trade deteriorated had only one way out, and that was to take advantage (as it seemed then) of rapidly increasing supplies of international money to promote continued investment. Then, three things happened together: most developing countries' export earnings fell away; the cost of their imports rose; and the price of current and outstanding credit to bridge the gap rose. Extreme indebtedness or drastic cutbacks in imports of consumer goods and industrial supplies were the only possible results; most countries suffered both. The instability of exchange rates led to massive speculative, followed by later outflows of capital, which intensified the need for external credit. International aid, which would have been some compensation, decreased in real terms even below promised levels.

The debt crisis became even more crucial. Private banks' exposure to the potential defaulting of indebted countries rose continually; coalitions of these heavily indebted countries met to demonstrate solidarity and wrest better terms from their creditors; and many countries rescheduled while a few unilaterally announced a moratorium on their debts. In 1985, growth faltered again to the accompaniment of protectionist measures. Restrictions were threatened indiscriminately against some developing as well as developed countries with trade surpluses whose only hope for economic recovery (assuming the world financial system didn't collapse) lay in increasing their export earnings over a long period.

The real cost of these strains on the international financial markets fell on the people, particularly the poorest. Falling wages, fewer jobs, and higher prices for basic goods ravaged the standard of living of millions already deep in poverty. As the crisis deepened and income distribution worsened starting in the early 1980s, women and children suffered most; as a graphic measure of the ultimate cost, infant mortality rates rose in poor families, reversing the historical trend.

As well as pessimism and uncertainty about the prospects for national development in many countries, there were grounds for concern that *women* were bearing the brunt of contemporary economic decline. That concern should now be properly translated into policy measures supported by the analytical framework. It should, among others, explore the relation between expansion of the international economy in the postwar period and changes in women's work and welfare. Given the importance of the international economy and its effect on women, the neglect of this dimension, compared with the wealth of case study material that now exists in women's and economic studies, is evident. The Nairobi Conference made it clear that there is a great need for work in this area, which, if neglected, could jeopardize the entire development process.

The topic is reminiscent of a question that influenced many women in development research in the 1970s. How were women's role affected by the monetization of less developed societies, that is, by the introduction of capitalist processes of commercialization and accumulation to remote agricultural communities, for example? The standard answer was that commercial activities were taken over by men, while women, who had previously been engaged in agriculture alongside men, became newly ensconced in domestic work. That is to say, under the circumstances, social relations of gender intensified the division of labor between the sexes, identifying men with the productive sphere and women with the reproductive sphere. Women came to concentrate on social reproduction, that is, on nurturing (male) entrants to the labor force, rather than in participating in gainful employment for themselves. Has this tendency continued with the growing dependence on international trade as opposed to local and national markets?

The only possible way at present of monitoring the sexual division of labor in an aggregative study such as this is to measure women's labor force participation, that is, their involvement in paid work. Given current statistical methods, comprehensive, comparative data do not exist from which to get a direct measure of unpaid household work burdens. But there are better reasons than statistical exigencies for concentrating on women's labor force participation. Despite its inadequacy as a measure of women's economic *contribution,* labor force participation does open up to women an area where a broader range of skills can be developed than in family and household labor. And, more importantly, women can earn and control their income, which is a first step toward economic emancipation. Monetary income is the indispensable means to economic power in monetized societies, and it enhances women's family and bargaining power and hence status. It is a necessary if not sufficient condition for women's emancipation.

As with all empirically based social research, the argument is shaped by the available evidence. It is far more difficult to identify employment trends, especially for women, than to monitor international trade and financial transactions. There continues to exist an imbalance in the quantity and quality of information available. Employment data are perhaps most flawed in all economic sectors, particularly in the informal sector, so the thread of the argument here is based on partial evidence.

Finally, time lags intensify the information imbalance. This study takes a long-term view of economic changes, emphasizing trends in patterns of female employment since the 1960s. Data are generated much more quickly about international economic transactions than about labor force and employment matters, publication taking as little as a few days or weeks in the former and as much as years in the latter. So while case study material is used wherever possible to elucidate current employment trends, information on that side of the equation is inevitably dated. The general conclusion of the study—that international factors have contributed to the rise in female paid employment and influenced the structure of work opportunities in women's favor—

should therefore not be taken without qualification to the present day. It is an evaluation of the long-term sweep of events up to the 1980s.

The innovative nature of *Women in the World Economy* is discussed in the Statement at the beginning of this book. Such a work often raises more questions than it answers. The present one, however, concludes with a number of research findings that lead to policy recommendations that could have far-reaching implications for governments and private and public enterprises as well as international corporations and organizations.

Women in the World Economy is not innovative in one important respect. It is a study that relies on the conventional tools of economic analysis applied to research and data that are already available. By taking this path, INSTRAW is advocating the need for change in current economic thinking on development. Such an approach does not dwell on the social and cultural implications of economic change for women. These are areas for future exploration, and they quite probably call not only for a different approach but also for new systems of research methodologies, conceptual analysis, and data collection.

2

The Position of Women in a Changing World

Has the quality of life improved for the citizens of the world in the forty years since the establishment of the United Nations? The founding purpose of the United Nations was to promote peace and prosperity throughout the world, on the basis of a "faith in fundamental human rights" that included "the equal rights of men and women." Did this aim come at all close to fruition? Have all the aid, investment, and commitment to development devoted to these ends been in vain? Have economic changes, whatever the causal role of the United Nations itself, brought about any diminution in the disparities in wealth and well-being between whole peoples and between men and women within and between countries?

Some aspects of the "quality of life" are measurable. One of the objectives of the United Nations itself was to improve and standardize the conceptual basis and collection of data of this kind, and so make it possible to estimate what progress was being made over time and what remained still to be done. In this respect certainly, the situation has improved, and national income and individual life chances data are now available worldwide. Although information is still inevitably partial, some comparisons across space and over time can be made.

Let us examine first the direct quality of life indicators. Presentation of the data broken down by sex makes it clear that significant differences by sex exist in each dimension. Life expectancy is arguably

12

the single most important measure of at least the *potential* quality of life. Longevity is an all-encompassing measure of health and economic standards: critical deficiencies in either of these variables may terminate life. Conversely, improvements in the base levels of each or both will result in an increase in the average life span of members of a particular society.

Health and Education

Life expectancy has risen dramatically in most, though not all, countries, in the postwar period (Sivard 1985). Average life expectancy increased from sixty-six to seventy-four years in the developed countries of North America, Europe, Japan, and Oceania and from forty-four to sixty-one years in the developing countries of Africa, Asia, and Latin America between 1950 and 1985. The remaining statistics on national life expectancy are shocking in view of the demonstrated ability of most human societies to increase longevity. Life expectancy has not risen at all in some countries in Africa and Asia; in Gambia, Guinea, and Sierra Leone it is still less than forty years according to United Nations Population Division 1986 estimates. In proportional terms, the improvement has been greatest in developing countries, but average life expectancy there has still not reached that prevailing in developed countries thirty-five years ago. An average citizen of one of the poorest countries in the world has a life expectancy only a little over half as long as an average citizen in one of the richest.

These differences in longevity are strongly associated with different levels of national income. The widest disparity is between the two broadest regional groupings in the world, developed and developing countries: per capita incomes were approximately $8,000 and $800, respectively, in 1980, and life expectancy was seventy-four and sixty-one years. Between the greatly varied continental regions of the developing world, the covariation is equally striking. South Asia and sub-Saharan Africa are the poorest regions by far, with incomes of about $220 and life expectancies of about fifty years, whereas East Asia, with incomes of about $1,000, and Latin America, with incomes of $2,000, have considerably higher levels of life expectancy of about sixty-five years.

Female life expectancy exceeds male life expectancy in almost all societies (though by a narrow margin in poorer regions and with a reverse differential in a few countries in Asia). In 1985, female life expectancy was estimated to be seventy-seven years in developed countries, seven years longer than for men. The sex difference in life expectancy appears to have widened over the years: in 1950, life expectancy was only five years greater for women than men in developed countries. The gender gap in longevity has also widened a little in middle-income developing countries but not yet elsewhere in the developing world (World Bank 1985).

The gap between male and female life expectancies is partly a reflection of genetic differences between the sexes and partly a reflection of social, cultural, and economic factors. Women's hormones protect them from atherosclerotic diseases; their lower metabolic rate and higher proportional body fat content may also make them less vulnerable to a range of other chronic and critical conditions. Increasingly, the most prevalent lethal diseases in developed countries are attributable to smoking and to the dietary habits associated with affluent lifestyles; women are less prone to these diseases than men, partly for genetic reasons and partly due to more moderate female consumption patterns. In some of the poorer countries, however, sexually distinct consumption patterns have the opposite outcome in terms of relative survival rates. In India, Nepal, and Pakistan, male life expectancy untypically *exceeds* the female level. The difference is attributable to the higher female mortality rate in two specific age ranges: among children aged one to five years and among adults younger than thirty-five years (in women, the childbearing years). The difference in childhood mortality rates is due to nutritional and medical neglect of girls compared with boys. There is a striking sex bias against women in the distribution of food and other commodities, such as hospital services, as shown by numerous studies (most but not all referring to the Indian subcontinent) (Sen 1985). At the levels of impoverishment prevailing in the Indian subcontinent, these shortfalls lead inexorably to higher morbidity and lower childhood and total life expectancies among women.

Although the world population approximately doubled in absolute numbers between 1950 and 1985, mainly because of falls in mortality rates, declining fertility has resulted in the rate of population increase slowing down. In terms of health and physical well-being, this has been specifically to women's advantage. The decrease has saved women from higher specific mortality rates during childbearing age in most countries. On average, the number of children born per woman fell between 1950 and 1985 from 2.8 to 2.0 in developed countries and from 5.9 to 3.8 in developing countries. There are again considerable variations between different regions of the developing world, however, ranging from 6.6 in sub-Saharan Africa to 4.7 in other parts of Africa, 4.2 in South Asia, 3.9 in Latin America, and 2.5 in the Far East (including Japan). The expected rates of total population growth in each of these regions in the last two decades of the twentieth century match this ranking, being highest in sub-Saharan Africa (3 percent a year between 1980 and 2000), much lower in Asia and in Latin America (2.1 percent), and lowest of all in the developed countries (0.4 percent). It is worth noting how drastically China, the most populous country and yet one of the countries with a low income per capita, has broken away from this trend: its population growth is estimated to be only 1.2 percent, well below that of other countries at the same income level.

High fertility causes low total life expectancy, partly because infant mortality rates are higher when births are frequent and narrowly spaced and partly because women's health and robustness are drained by repeated pregnancies and periods of lactation. The benefit to women's well-being from reduction of fertility, which permits women's genetically based greater potential longevity to emerge, should not be underestimated. Fertility decline, which comes from income increases supplemented by deliberate public efforts at family planning, is one of the most important specific benefits that general economic development has brought to women. Human life has been called nasty, brutish, and short, but reductions in fertility have made it both less brutish and less short for millions of women, though millions of others in many of the poorest developing countries are still suffering the effects of too-frequent childbirth. It has also been argued that high fertility rates are the root cause of women's limited role in public, social, economic, and political life. Modern contraception makes childbearing a matter of choice for the first time and removes reproductive capability as an excuse for discrimination against women in these matters (Stern 1985; Bryceson 1985).

Prospects for both men and women have also improved in regard to literacy and education, which also contribute in a major way to greater realization of human potential. Education is, moreover, a vital precondition for a fully productive life in the modern world. The picture of development since 1950 in this area in fact has some very positive features. But in this case women are firmly disadvantaged; there is considerable disparity in educational provision for men and women. Though improvements have been made, much remains to be done to bring about equality between the sexes.

Literacy rates among current population mainly reflect the education given to present adults as children. While there is no significant difference in literacy rates between men and women in the developed world, in developing countries only half the total female population is literate compared with sixty-eight percent of men. Variation levels and the gender gap in literacy and current educational provision within the developing world roughly match income levels. Thus, in Latin America, eighty-five percent of men and eighty-one percent of women are literate, whereas in Africa only fifty-seven percent of men and thirty-six percent of women are literate; in Asia (excluding China, for which information is not available) only sixty-five percent of men and forty-four percent of women are literate. In the poorest area of Asia, the Indian subcontinent, only fifty-six percent of men and thirty-one percent of women are literate. The match with income is not smooth, in that total average literacy levels are significantly higher in Asia than in Africa, though the income ranking is the reverse. But the gender gap—the difference in percentage points between male and female literacy levels—*does* follow the income ranking. Money evidently buys life *and* learning, especially for women.

School enrollment rates rose among both boys and girls at all levels and in all countries in the postwar period, marking a major social achievement. The situation is generally still much worse in developing than in developed countries. In the 1980s, six out of every ten girls aged five to nineteen in developing countries were *not* at school. There were more boys than girls attending at every level of education. But the gap has been narrowed, especially at the secondary level. Girls represented forty-four percent of primary, forty-one percent of secondary, and about thirty-three percent of third-level students in developing countries in 1985, compared with thirty-seven percent, twenty-four percent, and twenty-five percent in 1950. These improvements suggest that the literacy gap between the sexes will be reduced in future generations, and educational qualifications in general will improve, as indeed has happened in the developed countries (especially in regard to third-level qualifications) over the postwar period.

Economic Activity

Health and education are the main indicators of male and female social status. Economic status is the last but most causally important variable to be considered. It would be best to measure actual individual incomes, but this is extremely difficult to do in any comprehensive way for men and women separately given their membership in income-pooling households. Pooling means that no person's final benefits or rewards *necessarily* match their contribution to household income (though, as will be seen, there is an association). The best proximate indicator of individual incomes is the individual level of economic participation in recorded employment. Since education is the main route to more prestigious employment in the modern world, it is not surprising to find the gender gap in educational provision mirrored in lesser participation and lesser rewards in formal employment for women compared with men. But it is also the case that the rate of female economic activity in this sense has increased during the postwar period; it is more doubtful that their relative *rewards* have improved, though, as will be seen, there is some evidence in support of this proposition for women in the *developing* world.

The numbers of women in the labor force rose in both developed and developing countries between 1950 and 1985 in terms of both the proportion among all adult women carrying out (or seeking) paid employment and the share that these women represented of the labor force in total (ILO/INSTRAW 1985). In 1950, forty-nine percent of adult women in developed countries and thirty-seven percent of women in developing coutries were registered as belonging to the labor force; by 1985, the statistics had risen by eight and five percent to fifty-seven and forty-two percent, respectively. Over the same period, the numbers of men joining the labor force *fell* in relation to the total male population with increases in third-level and vocational educational enrollment, so that there was a rather more pronounced rise in the proportional importance of women in the whole labor force than the increases in the female participation rate implied. Whereas in 1950, women were thirty-eight percent of the total labor force in developed countries and twenty-eight percent in developing countries, by 1985 their shares had risen to forty-one and thirty-two percent, respectively. Women thus became increasingly visible over the years as providers of productive labor, but still by 1985 scarcely half as many women as men were in paid employment.

Regional variations in the rate of female labor force participation are worth noting. Women are almost as important in the labor force as men in the socialist countries of Eastern Europe, where male and female participation rates are very similar. Among other developed countries, the participation rate is particularly high in North America. At the other end of the scale lie the Middle East and North Africa, where women's participation is low and where it actually fell rather than rose with the local rise in income from increased oil revenues from the mid-1970s onwards. Cultural traditions in these areas have always limited the public role of women. The sudden increase in wealth allowed greater conformity with traditional ideas about women's "proper place," that is, concentrating on bearing children rather than participating in the labor force (the fertility rate in this region is very high and out of line with the rates for equivalent income levels elsewhere). In the 1980s, as part of a changing outlook in many countries, including the developed ones, there has been a resurgence of these traditional values. In Latin America too, cultural values discourage women's active participation in paid employment and hold down the official female participation rate, though it has been rising steadily (from twenty percent in 1950 to twenty-five percent in 1985). In most places in Asia and Africa, cultural values do not militate against allowing women a visible, productive role to the same extent, and variations in the female participation rate are correlated with income level. The rate is lowest in South Asia, where about thirty-six percent of women were in the formal labor force; next lowest in Africa, where the rate was forty-two percent; and highest in East Asia (excluding Japan) at fifty-two percent.

There are no comprehensive data on the earnings and rewards of female labor, but such evidence as exists consistently shows that in this respect women's experience of formal employment is inferior to men's. There is a persistent and substantial wage gap by sex. In sixteen developed countries in 1982, women's hourly earnings in manufacturing industry averaged less than three quarters of men's; they were slightly less than that in the nine developing countries in the sample (Sivard 1985). Comparable data are not available for agriculture and services. Much of this difference in earnings is attributable to the unequal distribution of male and female workers in different types of jobs according to their wage level; the female distribution is weighted toward the low-paid end of the job scale. But an increasing number of case studies show that even in job-for-job comparisons, women's earnings are usually less than men's. There is also mounting evidence that grading procedures are differentiated by sex, so that women's jobs are often classed as lower ranked in the occupational hierarchy than is in fact warranted. In so far as this is the case, the real earning differential by sex for equivalent work is in fact wider than official statistics indicate.

The occupational distribution of women workers reflects not only women's relative wages but also the inherent rewards and status of the work they do. Women are concentrated in low-skilled, repetitive work without formal responsibility in the organizations where they are employed and with far fewer prospects of promotion and advancement than male workers enjoy. In agriculture, where complementarity between cultivation tasking is intrinsic to the whole process and there is no command hierarchy as such, men tend to claim such advanced tools and machinery as are available and women are relegated to "tending" tasks such as planting, weeding, and threshing where these are still done by hand. There are far more male than female self-employed workers running their own enterprises and far more female than male unpaid family workers in such endeavors.

The ranking is more explicit in manufacturing industry and within the professional services. Women carry out most of the assembly line, manual-labor-intensive operations in industry, and they work as secretaries to managers, rather than as supervisors and managers themselves. In the services sector, women account for far higher proportions of nurses and paramedics than doctors and of primary than secondary and head school teachers. There is an echo here of women's relatively greater deprivation at higher levels of education; it has also been shown that the wage differential by sex increases with higher educational qualifications (Bryceson 1985). In terms of social evaluation and reward, women thus occupy subordinate positions. New entrants to the official labor force over the postwar period have remained confined in the main to such positions; they have not succeeded in penetrating "masculine" areas of work to any significant extent. The persistence of the pattern is suggested by the experience in Britain, where the degree of occupational segregation of this kind has been virtually unaltered for more than seventy years.

The insufficiency of official definitions of *productive work* as an indication of how people spend their time and the social value of what they do makes it tempting to discard the data on labor force participation and employment altogether. The ILO/INSTRAW study (1985), along with many other studies (e.g., Beneria [1981]; Anker [1983]), makes clear the need for new statistical definitions of employment. But the present data do have some merit. First, they signal an important fact of social organization. In ignoring household maintenance work, statisticians faithfully reflect the universal devaluation of subsistence activity. More substantively, it cannot be denied that the many improvements in the standard of living that have been achieved through history have fundamentally been due to advances in science and technology that have not been generated in the household sphere. Despite the indispensable contribution of household maintenance, the catalysts to material progress have come from elsewhere. As long as women remain confined to and identified with household work, their economic contribution will remain underrated, their contribution to material progress needlessly limited, and their civic autonomy undermined by their lack of access to money. Money matters because it is a route to the accumulation of wealth and power. Women's increased participation in the formal labor force as conventionally measured indicates that they are doing more work that is monetarily rewarded. (However, "unpaid family labor," in family enterprises, which does *not* include household maintenance work, is a form of formal labor force participation that may not receive monetary compensation in practice.) A rise in the rate at which women participate in the formal labor force, that is, in the proportional numbers of adult women who undertake or try to undertake paid work, thus generally signifies women's first step away from domesticated servility.

Or does it? The assumption of domestic duties by women could be more symptom than cause of women's weak political and social position in monetized societies (even though it can undoubtedly be regarded as the proximate cause at the microlevel of women's poor bargaining position when it comes to their entry into the paid labor market). Given that domestic work, unpaid, seems universally to be considered women's work, could it not be that it is women's work per se that is undervalued, whatever it happens to consist of? Merely stepping outside the home may not guarantee improved status. The fact that not *all* domestic servants are either unpaid or female hints at this possibility. "Domestic service" is after all a large occupational category within the bounds of officially recorded employment: many people are paid for doing it. Most of these workers are women employed by others beyond their immediate circle, but some are men (especially in Asia). In other words, a small proportion of all the women in the world carrying out domestic work are paid on a contractual basis, but all *men* who undertake work are paid for it.

There is much to be said for the notion that whatever work women do is devalued. As has been seen, women's rewards in paid employment seem to be systematically lower than men's in industry. And in rural settings, the fact that the operations at the top end of the agricultural chain—the final preparation of food crops to convert them to usable form—are unpaid, unlike the preceding cultivation tasks, can only be seen as arbitrary until it is recognized that the latter operations are done by women. But the fact remains that there is a crucial distinction in social and economic terms between work that receives a monetary reward and work that does not, regardless of whether the *level* of remuneration in the former case is in some sense appropriate or fair. Money, the general means of exchange, is of increasing significance with the monetization of the economics of even the most remote and materially deprived of societies. It is not surprising that the social valuation or, in Sen's terms (1985), the *perceived contribution* of labor effort should (perhaps increasingly) rest on its monetary equivalent as revealed in a direct money payment.

It is increasingly accepted that receipt of direct money earnings does indeed mark an improvement in status. Within the household, there are three reasons for this. Paid work is perceived to make a higher contribution to the family's channeling of money to the household and so goes along with a larger say in household decisions; also, payment of money can carry conversely a threat of withdrawal of that money, which gives the earner greater bargaining power within the household. Increased status confers better material provision, that is, increased claims on the share of consumer goods within the household, and so the link is established between employment status and economic benefit. Aggregative empirical analysis confirms this, in the shape of the contrast between Africa and Asia, between Southeast Asia and South Asia, and between South and North India, for example, where in each case the relative material position of women is better in the first place than in the second, in association with a higher rate of female participation in the recorded labor force. Numerous case studies also point to the importance of outside employment in improving the treatment that women get in society in general and in the household in particular (Sen 1985). The role of outside employment, with its acknowledged productive status, in raising the position of women thus can scarcely be overemphasized.

The female labor force participation rate as the measure of women's economic status is thus arguably the key one of the various indicators of the quality of life for women. But all the indicators are powerfully associated with levels of *national* income. The broad picture of economic and social development has been toward slight, but perceptible, reductions in the gender gap in health, educational, and economic status on the one hand and toward, until recently, steady growth in national incomes and material provision on the other. The relationship broadly obtains spatially (between regions and countries at any given date) as well as over time. The message of all the data is thus fundamentally an optimistic one from women's point of view—though it is also very clear that if national income is taken simplistically as the only determinant of women's status, then full equality between the sexes is still a very long way off.

Macroeconomic-Microeconomic Links

International economic relations have been a major influence on economic growth and material progress in both developed and developing countries during the postwar period, and the international economy is inescapably important when it comes to analyzing what has happened in the most recent past, since the mid-1970s. A relatively favorable run of economic events came indisputably to an end with the world recession of the 1980s. Up to that time, global income increased faster than population, so that in principle the standard of living of all the world's population could rise year by year. There were regional variations in this average, of course, but almost every single country, even the poorest, managed some increase, however small. Things have been very different since 1980. There has been outright economic decline, unprecedented for a generation, in many countries. Whole continents have experienced falls in their collective real income per capita, Africa by a little more than 2 percent and Latin America by fully 3.6 percent a year on average between 1981 and 1984 (World Bank 1985). Other developing countries, mostly in Asia, have seen their rate of growth checked but continue to grow at rates higher than those obtaining in the developed countries, so they are quite rapidly closing the income gap between themselves and at least the weakest of the richer countries. Hence, along with the reversals in some areas has come increasing disparity *within* the developing world. The fundamental economic health of the industrialized countries themselves has also come to be seen as far more uncertain than it seemed twenty or even fifteen years earlier, and the recovery heralded by some in the mid-1980s is extremely hesitant and uncertain, especially in the largest of all economies, the United States. These generalized difficulties and the essential character of the world recession cannot be understood without reference to the international dimension.

This raises the obvious question, in relation to economic and social development and sexual equality, as to the impact of the international economy—in both its positive and negative features—on the status of women: To what extent are the (modest) improvements in women's status in the past forty years specifically attributable to international economic factors? How, by extension, are women likely to be affected by the internationally determined recessionary downturn that started in 1980? Even when the data on the quality of life of men and women for this period become available, the question will still remain as to what the nature and mechanisms of the impact of international economic relations on women's economic status, and in particular on female employment, have been. These are the topics on which we will concentrate henceforth.

What has been the fate of women in this regressionary situation? If income increases generally bring improvements in women's status, as the data broadly suggest, do *reversals* worsen their condition within their own societies, so that they suffer disproportionately in periods of declining income?

The divergent economic prospects of different developing countries since 1980 are explicable in terms of international economic relations. The course of economic development and material progress in all countries, especially poorer ones, has in fact been heavily contingent on the impact of the international economy—in both its positive and negative features—and the nature of individual countries' involvement in international markets in the postwar period. To what extent are the (modest) improvements in women's status in the past forty years *specifically* attributable to international economic factors? And how, by extension, are women likely to be affected in the internationally determined recessionary downturn that started in 1980?

The broad argument of this study is twofold. First, it will be shown that the international dimension has become an increasingly important element of the total economic environment for all countries during the postwar period, such that growth and development, while not wholly determined by international factors, cannot be explained without reference to them. There have been major changes in the institutions governing international markets in goods, services, and money, and the volume of transactions in these markets has grown increasingly faster than transactions within national markets. Technological changes utilized internationally have also greatly increased the productivity of many economic activities. Individuals' and countries' potential for economic production and consumption has been greatly modified as a result. Second, the international economy *has* had a differential impact on the employment of men and women and has specifically influenced women's economic status as a result. The differential impact has followed from the fact that both within and across sectors of economic activity, there are distinctive male and female patterns of activity. The effects on women of changes in international economic relations have not been monolithic, but some systematic tendencies can be identified. Outcomes have roughly followed certain trends by major region.

The broad principle of allocation of economic activities between men and women can be characterized as following the power of men to preempt prime economic activities for themselves. What is *prime* in this sense varies from society to society and from time to time, so that the sexual division of labor is never absolutely fixed in terms of specific activities. Furthermore, the *scope* for women's participation in the formal economy is residual, rising potentially with increases in the resources available to a population. The ratio itself is not fixed in physical terms but is a function of prevailing technology determining the level of social productivity.

It is both possible and feasible to trace the impact of changes in the international environment in these terms on a sectoral basis, though even at this level of disaggregation the trends are far from neat. In agriculture, there is a complex picture of sometimes counteracting tendencies at work. Internationally diffused technologies have in some places and for some crops enormously increased the productivity of land and thus effectively expanded the resource base and with it the employment opportunities for female labor. But they have also had the secondary effect of causing changes in methods of production that have modified the proportional number of primary and casual or secondary employment positions. Thus, the effects of the "green revolution" for women have varied over time: at first, total demand for all labor (including female) rose, but later female labor has tended to be displaced. In places where international technology has had no local impact, agricultural populations have felt its effect indirectly through trade, very greatly to their disadvantage as producers. International influences have predominantly depressed relative returns from previously "female" activities, confirming the preexisting sexual division of labor. But this same phenomenon has also effectively introduced a trend toward greater population pressure on land resources, thus reducing the scope for female participation. In industry, trends have been clearer, and female activity has been doubly expanded by international influences. International economic integration has increased both the net number of secondary employment positions and the industrial resource base—and thus the scope of female employment; these changes have been especially important to women in the developing countries. In some parts of the service sector, similar trends to those in industry have prevailed, increasing female employment; in others, the international economy has had only an indirect effect on female employment through its influence on the general configuration of the economy. In Latin America, the service sector is particularly important in employment terms (especially for women) partly because, in both agriculture and industry, relatively capital-intensive structures were built up, which on the one hand discriminated against female employment and on the other were uncompetitive internationally and help to explain the continent's dismal economic performance since the late 1970s. International pressures have resulted in widespread impoverishment in the region, which has both generated a demand for more subsidiary labor in industry and services and increased the supply of women prepared to take on employment of this kind. All these various sectoral developments are explained in greater detail in the chapters that follow.

These same observations can also be made at the regional level because the distribution of sectoral activities differs by continent. In Asia industry has been the most dynamic economic sector, and female employment has expanded because of international influences. In Africa, where agriculture predominates, international trade rather than technological factors have been active, and prices have fallen while productivity (with its mixed effects for women) has scarcely changed over the years. The situation is becoming increasingly disadvantageous to women because the main result has been to add to the already emerging pressure of a growing population on the land. Finally, in Latin America, the services sector is the largest, and it has been mostly indirectly affected by the international economy by way of the widespread impoverishment resulting from international pressures since the late 1970s. The level of female employment has probably been increased in this case but on appallingly bad terms, which makes it difficult to hold (as nevertheless we must) that the rise in female labor force participation is beneficial to women even in the most adverse circumstances.

As this analysis suggests, the divergences in regional economic prospects within the developing world since the mid-1970s have to a

large extent been causally associated with the respective sectoral patterns of activity. In order to understand the local impact of international economic relations, it is necessary first to describe the postwar changes in the economic environment and to demonstrate their increasing importance at the sectoral and national levels. Only after that can we show how the various international markets have interacted to cause the world recession that began in 1980.

Historical Perspective

Forty years is an apposite period to take for this examination. Immediately after the Second World War, as enlightened policy makers took stock of the socioeconomic disaster of the 1930s' Great Depression, which had done so much to lay the foundations of the war itself, institutions and mechanisms were established to open up relations and increase international trade and economic stability. The setting up of the United Nations itself was also very much part of this movement. The depth and international scope of the depression had been greatly increased by the restrictions on trade introduced by the major nations (especially in the notorious Hawley-Smoot Tariff introduced by the United States), in a misguided effort to protect their own industries. Sparked off by such measures, the value of world trade had fallen by about two thirds in the four years after 1929. The central principle of the postwar arrangements made at the Bretton Woods Conference in 1944 was to reestablish trade and currency convertibility so as to ensure that international economic exchanges could not ever again be disrupted to the same extent.

International trade and financial flows *have* been reestablished and liberalized since the Bretton Woods institutions—the International Monetary Fund and the World Bank—were set up forty years ago. A third organization was proposed (to be called The International Trade Organization) but never agreed to. As it happened, the General Agreement on Tariffs and Trade (GATT) performed some of its intended functions. These agencies and the GATT were later joined by the United Nations Conference on Trade and Development with the special mandate to advocate trade and related improvements for developing countries. Tariffs have been brought down and mechanisms for the regulation of trade and resolution of disputes agreed to and internationally respected in the main. Financial markets have expanded more than enough to finance the increased trade, though the institutional arrangements here are less coherent and securely based.

But these were only the facilitating conditions. Other developments have been just as important in increasing the incentives and ability for international trade. Technological progress has been one such factor. Improvements in shipping, air transport, and means of communication over long distances have allowed far more goods of different kinds to be traded than ever before and goods to travel further and faster. Telecommunications lie behind the emergence of a new form of industrialization, the transnational corporation, which has been responsible for much of the increase in trade in manufactured goods in this period. More fundamentally, the reconstruction and investment that led to widespread expansion of productive capacity from the 1950s onward among the developed countries was based on financial grants transferred to Europe by the United States under the Marshall Plan. Recovery and growth were strong, and the industrialized countries experienced a period of unprecedented high growth between 1948 and 1971. All the major countries (with the exception of the United States itself) achieved faster growth of industrial output during this time than for the previous eighty years. The quantity of goods being produced and available for trade was thus increasing rapidly all the time. As the benefits of specialization through trade were realized, investment patterns were modified, and the growth potential of these economies was enhanced still further in a virtuous circle. The process of trade liberalization was a slow one—so many trade restrictions had been in place that it necessarily took time to dismantle them. The impetus through trade to investment and growth was therefore periodically renewed through the years with each successive round of tariff reductions negotiated under the GATT. Some countries, notably in East Asia but also Latin America, also received financial support, primarily again from the United States, which enabled them to build up their capacity in industry and agriculture. These countries subsequently also began to exploit the potential of international markets, expanding the role of the less developed countries beyond that of mere suppliers of agricultural and mineral raw materials. From the 1970s, the growth of the newly industrializing countries' exports has exceeded that of developed countries.

Small countries have always had a greater interest and incentive to trade than larger. If they limit production to their own market, they cannot take full advantage of economies of scale. This consideration becomes more important with industrialization, because scale economies are more common in manufacturing than in agricultural activities. The spread of industrialization in many parts of the developing world in the postwar period therefore in itself provided something of an impetus to trade expansion.

Moreover, economies of scale seem to be becoming more important *within* industry, as new products are invented and new processes evolve that require enormous capital investment and the need to generate huge revenues not achievable from any single national market. The emergence of electronics is the most striking example (although some parts of the electronics industry are carried out on a smaller scale). Such operations have added to trade flows in one (or both) of two ways. In some cases, the process of production is spread out internationally, usually under the aegis of transnational corporations, with some operations located far from the company base to take advantage of international differences in factor costs: the geographical separation generates flows of goods in intermediate as well as final stages of fabrication. Second, scale economies are conducive to intraindustry trade and specialization. Different countries establish a facility to meet slightly different types of consumer demand within a given product category, while in each national market broadly similar sets of consumer preferences require supply of the whole range of products. Intraindustry international specialization of this kind leads to cross-trade in only slightly differentiated final products.

The increasing importance of economies of scale in production has reinforced the potential gains for individual countries from specialization from trade. As the framework of the international exchange of goods has been improved in the postwar period, more and more countries—large and small, developed and developing—have been able to take advantage of trade. Virtually all countries now have higher levels of imports and exports than before, though the proportional importance of trade in their economies does still vary by size. The largest countries outside the European socialist bloc, the United States, China, and Brazil, have roughly doubled their exports in proportion to their total output in the past twenty years to around ten percent. Almost all other countries (the only exceptions being a number of the poorest developing countries) have also increased their exports, if not to the same degree (because not from such low base). In 1982, almost one fifth of the total output of the developed countries combined was exported, compared with twelve percent in 1960; trade was even more important to many developing countries, with middle-income countries increasing their exports from seventeen to twenty-three percent over the same period (World Bank 1984a).

World trade, growing at over seven percent annually between 1948 and 1971, consequently outstripped the growth of the total output of the nine largest developed market economies, which grew at less than five percent over that period (Griffith-Jones 1983). The previous high rate of increase for a comparable length of time was in the middle of the nineteenth century, when trade grew at 5.5 percent. In volume terms, the amount of goods exchanged has increased many times over: between about 1960 and the late 1970s, by more than six times in the case of manufactures and by about three times in the case of primary products (Batchelor, Major, and Morgan 1980). From 1950 to 1972 or so, the industrialized countries' exports grew faster than others', so that they gradually increased their share of world exports; however, after 1973 the picture was reversed and developing countries' trade performance was superior and their market share rose, in both manufactures and primary products.

The huge increases in the exchange of goods and services across national boundaries over the past forty years are only one part of the general trend toward international economic integration in this period. Two other arenas of exchange have emerged to complement the trade in tangible products and services: finance and technology. The latter provides the know-how for increased production and productivity in the productive sectors. The former provides the means of foreign currency payment for goods and services acquired abroad, and its function extends to the provision of capital for investment and credit. The astronomical increase in the international supply of finance has been perhaps the single most notable development of the postwar period.

Each of the postwar decades has seen a different major source of international capital flow appear. Immediately postwar, the United States was the wellspring through the Marshall Plan. In the 1950s, private corporations supplied most of the capital to developing countries for investment in wholly owned industrial plants, mines, and plantations; in many countries this capital enabled the first steps to be taken toward industrialization. The 1960s were the heyday of official development assistance (international aid), with the United States again playing a predominant role. In the 1970s, private banks emerged for the first time as a major channel for international financial transfers. Private international financial transfers increased by about twenty percent each year, considerably faster, even allowing for inflation, than the growth in the volume of total world trade. The nominal value of capital flow increased more than ten times between the beginning and the end of the decade, from about $9 billion in around 1970 to $115 billion in 1980 (Griffith-Jones 1983). Developing countries were the destination for about sixty percent of the total amount. The increase in financial flow has not ceased to grow exponentially since then, and it has been estimated that international financial flow now exceeds the value of total world transactions by a factor of twenty ($40 trillion as against $2 trillion [Schuh 1985]). Therefore, the international financial market now dwarfs the goods and services market in size.

It is not possible to quantify the scale of the international market in technology, the other main dimension of international economic exchange, but it seems that there has been a great increase in transactions here also. The level of "state of the art" technological know-how for a whole range of economic activities has escalated almost beyond recognition, with continued progress in pure and applied science in the industrialized countries over the past forty years. In agriculture, whole generations of new high-yielding plant varieties have been developed, and new chemical fertilizers and pesticides have been made available. In manufacturing, automation, computer-based numerically controlled procedures, and design techniques and engineering to unprecedented degrees of precision have become possible through advances in electronics; new biotechnology, for example, allows "artificial" production of foodstuffs as well as improved drug production. Electronics also has revolutionized certain services, notably telecommunications and the handling and processing of information.

The stock of technological knowledge available for international transfer has been enormously magnified. The facilities for the trading (i.e., for the transfer and diffusion) of technology have also improved both institutionally and with respect to physical capability. Radical improvements in transportation and communication have allowed materials embodying new technology and persons skilled in their application to travel faster and farther than ever before. More importantly perhaps, the growth of transnational corporations and consulting firms, in agribusiness as well as in mining and manufacturing, and the emergence of a vast network of bilateral and multilateral aid and technical assistance agencies have provided new channels for commercial and noncommercial technology transfer between nations. The establishment of a network of new multilaterally funded agricultural research and development organizations has been perhaps the single most notable development. The great increase in productivity experienced in many activities across all economic sectors (from which poorer countries have not been entirely excluded though their average productivity remains relatively low) is at root attributable to and symptomatic of enhanced international technology transfers over the past forty years.

In the following chapters, how female employment has been affected in different sectoral activities is examined. Recent international economic events have clearly set the regional scene against which to consider women's economic situation. The Asian economies are in general performing well: to what extent have women played a part in their success and shared in the benefits of growth? In the context of Latin America and Africa, however, the question is a different one: have women borne the brunt of economic stagnation and decline? These questions are examined further in the following chapter.

Part II

THE CHANGING INTERNATIONAL ECONOMIC ENVIRONMENT

Part II

THE CHANGING INTERNATIONAL ECONOMIC ENVIRONMENT

3

Trade and Finance

The Growth and Composition of Trade

The long-term trend in international exchanges over the past forty years has been in the consolidation and expansion of product and financial markets to an unprecedented degree. That these markets are not separate but intimately connected is shown by events occurring during the past fifteen years or so. The comparatively rapid and unproblematic growth of many economies came to an abrupt end in the early 1970s, and the period since then has been one of great turbulence. The resilience of national economies and indeed of the international economic system itself has been sorely tested in some respects. There have been two world recessions (not so far rivaling the 1930s' Great Depression in their scale, however). One of their most notable effects has been the polarization of the economic performance and prospects of different regional groupings of developing countries. Some have done well and have continued to experience the world's fastest rates of economic growth despite short-lived hiccups. Others have not and have entered a period of absolute decline with no end in sight: the implications are dreadful for millions of the world's poorest people. The economic situation of women in these different regions of the world has also been systematically and differentially influenced by international developments. To some extent, women have inevitably shared in the different fortunes of their respective countries and regions.

Before considering what the international economic events of the recent past have been and how they have affected women in different regions, we need first to describe the evolution of institutions and trade flow in international goods and financial markets. The main features have been the relatively faster growth of trade in manufactured goods than in other goods over the long period: faster growth of north to north trade than in north to south or south to south trade until 1973; extreme price rises for some primary commodities, namely petroleum; great fluctuations in some others and steady decline in the remainder; and the fastest growth of all in the scale of financial transactions. The emergence of transnational corporations with linked operations worldwide has contributed to the increased trade in manufactures, and changes in international payment arrangements in the early 1970s set the scene for the explosive growth of capital markets and of international debts of developing countries. While the developing countries taken as a single group remain a minor partner in the world economy, their share in various international markets has increased since the early 1970s. But their good aggregate performance conceals great disparities between individual developing countries and is due only to the exceptionally strong performance of some Asian economies as well as the strengthened position of oil exporters.

The expansion of the international goods trade has had as its core the rapid growth of trade in manufactures throughout the postwar period. The volume of manufactured goods traded has consistently grown faster, year by year, than both total trade and industrial output (and of course also than national output). The trend rates of growth of both output and exports of manufactures fell by about half around 1973 but the relation between the two has remained. World output of manufactures grew at seven percent annually while trade in manufactures increased at 11 percent from 1963 to 1973; from 1973 to 1980, output grew at 3.5 percent, trade at 5 percent. Since 1980, however, total trade has not increased at even this lower rate: after increasing by 3.5 percent in 1981, manufactures trade *fell* absolutely by 2.3 percent in 1982 (World Bank 1984a).

Developed market countries supply the bulk of all goods traded on world markets (sixty-three percent of all world exports in 1982 and

sixty-nine percent of goods traded outside the centrally planned economies of eastern Europe). Since the historical pattern of trade persists to a great extent with peripheral countries exporting primary products and metropolitan ones exporting industrial goods, it is not surprising that the share of developed countries in exports of manufactured goods is considerably higher, currently about eighty-three percent, than their share of total goods traded. Their predominance means that the postwar expansion of international trade in manufactures has rested on increased supply of exports by developed countries, which derived in turn from their rapid growth for the first two decades of the postwar period. Until 1973, developed countries' exports of manufactures were not only by far the larger part of world exports but grew faster than those of other regions. Since then, however, the most buoyant element has been the supply of manufactures by developing countries. Developing countries achieved an average rate of growth of manufactured exports of 10.6 percent in volume from 1973 to 1980, compared with a total increase from all sources of only 5 percent (World Bank 1984a). In the 1980s, the developing countries have also experienced the downturn in manufactured trade, to a lesser extent: in 1982, the volume of developing countries' manufactured exports declined by 1.6 percent (compared with the 2.3 percent fall in total world manufactured exports), after increasing by fully 16.3 percent in 1981; in 1983 they picked up again by 6 percent (World Bank 1984a).

Industrial goods traded internationally can be classified into two main product groups: capital goods (machinery and equipment, including transport equipment) and consumer and intermediate goods, of which textiles and clothing are the largest single item. Capital goods account for just under half of all industrial goods traded between market economies (forty-six percent in 1984). But different regions accounted for very different shares of these various product categories. Developed countries supply the overwhelming share of world exports of capital goods (ninety-two percent) and a much smaller—but notably still the majority—share of textiles and clothing (fifty-two percent). They also supply the bulk of all other miscellaneous manufactures (eighty-one percent). Developing countries are most prominent as suppliers of textiles and clothing and certain other light industrial products, mostly consumer goods (with the important exception of electronics components). The specialization of trade flow between developed and developing countries thus extends beyond the distinction between primary commodities and other goods to apply within the category of manufactures in ways of great significance to female employment.

The preponderance of textiles and clothing in the set of products exported by developing countries is the main feature. Footwear is added to these two in many official statistics; it is a minor category against the first two. Textiles, clothing, and footwear together accounted for thirty-seven percent of developing countries' exports in 1975, though by 1981 the proportion had fallen to twenty-six percent (World Bank 1985). They are more important as sources of export earnings to the poorer developing countries, accounting for forty-two percent of low-income, as against twenty-three percent of middle-income, developing countries' manufactured exports in 1981. Other major export product groups are electronics components and finished products, which together accounted for about six percent of manufactured exports at the beginning of the 1980s. There is also a miscellaneous batch of consumer goods, such as plastic and rubber goods, toys, sports goods, and watches. The countries that have achieved the fastest growth of exports of manufactures—a set of countries commonly called the newly industrializing countries (NICs), most of which are in East Asia—all have the capacity to export electronics products and tend also (though this is not true in all cases) to export a lower proportion of textiles and garments than the average. But whether from richer or poorer developing countries, the majority of manufactured goods exported are produced by work forces that include large numbers of women. The expansion of developing countries' exports of manufactures has in fact provided one of the main sources of new employment for women in the developing countries and is a distinctive feature of the impact of the evolution of the international economy on female employment.

The international prices of manufactures have not shown any dramatic changes during the postwar period. They have risen steadily throughout, except for a short-lived plateau in 1975 and 1976. This means that countries that export manufactures have had relatively stable foreign currency earnings, rising somewhat more than in proportion to the volume of such exports. Theirs was an enviable situation in comparison with that of countries that depended on exports of nonfuel primary products in particular.

Trade in manufactures has been influenced by institutional factors of two kinds, operating respectively to encourage and inhibit trade. The emergence of the transnational corporation and of other types of contractual cooperation between firms in different countries has stimulated trade; the creeping protectionism of recent years has inhibited it, undermining the advances made under the GATT to liberalize trading regulations.

Transnational Corporations

Transnational corporations (TNCs) have long been active in manufacturing in developing countries. Until the 1960s, they were limited to manufacturing operations that more or less duplicated those in the home country. Plants were set up to gain access to markets otherwise blocked by import restrictions, to supply goods for which proximity to the final market was important (because of high transport costs), or to make use of local raw materials. The production by TNCs of automobiles, agricultural engineering products, and pharmaceuticals spread far and wide among developing countries, are examples. For scale efficiency reasons of one kind or another, the main producing firms tend to be very large and to operate on a global scale in all of these industries. This kind of manufacturing production still predominates in the large Latin American countries that were the main sites for TNCs' overseas production facilities in this early phase. The manufacturing sector in these countries is still dominated by transnationals to a greater extent than in other regions: in the mid-1970s, to take the extreme case, almost one half of Brazil's industrial output was produced by transnationals and more than ninety-five percent of TNC production was sold locally. Characteristically then, this type of TNC activity did not have major implications for trade; developing country subsidiary plants would normally import some critical components from the parent company, but the bulk of the manufacturing effort was done locally, either in-plant, or, as developing country governments increasingly required, through purchase of locally produced inputs.

TNC involvement in developing countries has taken a new turn since then, in a type of production arrangement known as "global sourcing." Many complex production activities are broken down into a number of steps that need not be adjacent to one another—indeed, can be oceans apart. Some production stages may be heavily capital intensive, others highly labor intensive, with, in the extreme case, the work merely consisting of the assembly and testing of brought-in materials. There is little possibility of physical separation of product sites in continuous-process industries, but many light industrial processes do have the potential for separation, all that is required being that the components in various stages of fabrication be transportable between sites. Postwar improvements in transportation and telecommunications have vastly increased the scope, and reduced the cost, of long-distance fragmentation of production. There is an incentive to firms to disperse production sites internationally even when the final product is destined for the home market because absolute factor costs vary greatly between countries. Exchange rate fluctuations since the early 1970s have further increased the cost-saving potential of dispersing production internationally. In particular, there is an enormous spread in wage levels internationally, and the potential savings from locating labor-intensive processes in developing countries are very large. As one illustration, the shoe industry faces labor costs of $6 an hour in the United States and between $0.85 and $1.39 an hour in East Asia; in many developing countries, the wage rate would be even lower.

One industry in particular that has exploited the potential of global sourcing to the extreme—has in fact emerged on the back of this phase of the internationalization of capital—is the electronics components and consumer products industry. This industry has two crucial characteristics that have been conducive to the international spread of operations. Despite its high total average technology and capital intensity, the production of many electronic products falls into discrete segments, with some very labor-intensive processes involved. In principle, some of the operations involved could be automated, but paradoxically the very speed of scientific advance in this field has made it uneconomic in practice. The extremely short product cycles prevalent in electronics mean that it is not cost effective to undertake expensive tooling up for each new product (Eisold 1984); human labor has the strong advantage of flexibility in learning new procedures. The compactness of electronics parts and components means they can be transported internationally relatively cheaply. Also, the enormous research and development expenditures required of firms to survive in an industry with rapid innovation and volatile demand predisposes firms to be very large and, therefore, able to finance and manage the complex business of coordinating production in plants dispersed throughout the world. Electronics firms all sell to many different national markets, and competitive survival requires them to have globally planned production and sales strategies. Electronics TNCs carry out most of their labor-intensive production operations in developing countries. In the early 1970s, almost forty percent of employees of United States electronics firms were in developing countries (UNIDO 1981).

There is another twist to electronics and other TNCs' location of labor-intensive operations in developing countries. The cheapness of labor is the fundamental attraction when these locational decisions are made, although other financial and nonfinancial considerations of course enter in, for example, the local tax structure, the subsidies on start-up and other costs offered by the host government, and the political stability of the area. Cheapness of labor entails a whole host of variables apart from the crude wage rate that together determine total unit labor costs. The reliability of supply of labor, the level of education of the working population, and the prevailing rates of absenteeism and turnover are some such factors.

Electronics TNCs have not only located virtually all of their assembly operations in developing countries, but they have systematically preferred women workers. Around eighty percent of the electronics work force is female. It is often said that this is because Asian women have "nimble fingers"—that TNC plants that are mostly, though not all, in East Asia, employ women by preference. Their dexterity may make women especially valuable as employees, but it is much more likely that their low unit cost—and the availability of a large supply of well-educated workers, women as well as men, unusual for developing countries—had the largest weight in determining the TNCs' preference. Women's asking wage is lower for a start, and women have the social characteristics that make them the cheapest labor. The electronics industry is perhaps the most feminized of all modern manufacturing industries; TNCs perhaps came in without the cultural inhibitions against employing women that affect some local employers and in this sense were able to behave more rationally in seeing the profit-maximizing potential of an almost all-female work force (ILO/UNCTC 1985).

The availability of male labor in many of the developing countries where TNCs (not necessarily electronics firms) operate testifies to a systematic preference among TNCs for female labor. Even in some regions where the age of marriage and of first childbirth is so low that a sizable cohort of unmarried childless women is not available on the labor market, for example, in Haiti and other Caribbean countries, the preference for women remains; older women, whose children have grown, are employed instead of the younger, usually better educated, men among whom the rate of open unemployment is very high in these societies. That is, it is women workers' gender rather than their marital status that determines their distinctiveness. The sex wage differential is large enough in all societies to make women attractive to the cost-minimizing employer.

The importance of TNCs is evident in relation to trade. The new type of transnational involvement in internationally fragmented production processes has an inevitable corollary in adding to the amount of internationally traded manufactures, partly in the form of intermediates, partly in finished products. More than eighty percent of electronics products made in developing countries are exported, for example. Though it is difficult to assess what proportion of total trade in manufactures takes place between different parts of global corporations—and estimates vary—a recent estimate is that one half of all developing countries' manufactured exports consist of intrafirm trade (Taylor 1982). The definition of *intrafirm* is fairly wide, covering any two enterprises in different countries linked by ownership above a minimum level but not necessarily one hundred percent: the estimate therefore goes beyond intra-TNC trade, properly speaking. The bulk of the intrafirm trade flow is probably of movement of goods in varying stages of completion between fully incorporated plants belonging to a single centrally run corporation. The expansion of "sourcing" activities by transnationals using largely female labor must, in this perspective, have contributed significantly to the rapid growth of manufactured exports from developing countries.

There are many developing country exporting industries, however, where transnational corporations are *not* involved at both ends and where international cooperation between firms, while not altogether absent, is not the rule. Institutional links here take the form of "international subcontracting" between independent enterprises not more than one of which is a TNC (and probably neither); trade is only classed as "intrafirm" if there is an equity stake involved as well. This is the main form of international involvement of firms in the clothing industry, for example. Even so, internationally subcontracted goods accounted for only ten percent of United States and seventeen percent of West German imports of clothing from developing countries in 1974 (Joekes 1982b). The great bulk of developing country clothing exports are by autonomous local firms. Nevertheless, the worldwide geographical distribution of production capacity in these products has been changing quickly. Moreover, production capacity is now located in the developing countries while consumption has remained centered in the industrial countries. The divergence in the distribution of production and consumption has been reconciled through trade. Developing countries' increasing international competitiveness in these products has been based primarily on labor costs, and again female labor is the main type used. It is not an exaggeration therefore to say that developing countries' rapid growth of manufactured exports, on which the prosperity of the fastest growing countries has depended, lies in their specialization and comparative advantage in products made by women.

Constraints to Trade in Industrial Products

The strong showing that developing countries' manufactured exports made up to 1980 might seem to suggest that their future prospects are fairly good. But whether in fact conditions in the world market for industrial goods, and conditions specifically in the industrialized countries, which purchase sixty-three percent of developing countries' exports of manufactures, will be as favorable in the future as in the 1960s and 1970s is debatable. The developing countries entered international markets for manufactures in a big way at an extraordinarily propitious time in historical terms: the incomes of developed countries were growing at unprecedented rates, and international markets were expanding more rapidly than ever before. Since 1980, the trade situation has deteriorated considerably, with, in 1982, the first absolute fall in the volume of manufactures traded in decades. Future growth in trade and developing countries' prospects depend largely—though not entirely, in view of the increasing amount of trade *between* developing countries themselves—on recovery in demand in the industrialized countries. Moreover, as a reflection of industrialized countries' domestic industries' difficulties, access for developing countries' exports has been increasingly restricted in recent years.

There is much creeping protectionism in the 1980s. The principles of free trade instilled by the Bretton Woods institutions as an active ingredient of international economic relations on the whole continue to be observed; the lessons of the 1930s' Great Depression and the associated trade war are too clear to be set aside. Nontariff restrictions have been introduced on all sides with the hope they would not provoke general retaliation. These roundabout measures, ranging from administrative go-slows to quotas or "voluntary export restraints" (sometimes, as in the case of some European Economic Community (EEC) clothing imports regulations, even kept secret between the parties in a vain attempt to conceal their existence from others), are difficult to measure but do seem to have been becoming more widespread: it has been estimated that in 1983, twenty-two percent of world imports were subject to restrictions. Moreover, developing countries face more barriers on their exports to industrial countries than do industrial countries trading with one another, and they have relatively more restrictions on their manufactured products (Nogues, Olechowski, and Winters 1985). The original purpose of the General System of Preferences sponsored by UNCTAD, which introduced the principle of trade preferences *in favor* of developing countries (Greenhill 1984), has been overturned by these developments. In 1979, thirty percent of developing country manufactured imports into Organization for Economic Cooperation and Development (OECD) countries were subject to regulation, compared with eleven percent of imports from other OECD countries (Page 1981). In other words, when market conditions are tight, as they have been recently, developing countries are significantly discriminated against in acccess to the rich country markets that are the destination of most of their exports. This makes their better export performance than the industrialized countries since 1973 all the more remarkable, but it does also suggest that the industrialized countries are in effect taking steps to ensure that this export expansion is contained in the future.

Trade restrictions vary in their incidence among products. It is mostly in non-TNC-produced goods categories that neoprotectionist quotas and other nontariff barriers have been applied. Textiles and garments have been notoriously the most subject to chronic restrictions on entry to developed country markets. International specialization of production between developed and developing countries in these areas has not been directed by rich country industrial interests but has largely conflicted with them. TNC sourcing in electronics has been carried to its logical extreme for three reasons: there was little conflict of interest where new capability was involved that could be set up abroad right from the start; where any rundown of plant was entailed, the decision was internal to the organization that saw increased total global profits in the move; and TNC head offices continued to be based in the rich countries and had political access to the process of trade policy formulation, which allowed them to influence provisions in their product areas in their favor. Thus, the United States Trade Commission from early on reduced import duties on goods fabricated abroad by American companies compared with duties on imports made wholly abroad with no American involvement. In this perspective, the market advances developing countries have made in other product areas have been below their potential if trade had been fully free; developing countries' manufactured goods production would in all likelihood have increased even faster in the absence of trade restrictions.

Commodity Trade

The primary commodity sector's heterogeneity has become extremely pronounced in relation to international trade during the postwar period. The disparate trading conditions of four separate groups of primary products need to be distinguished in relation to the impact of the international economy on women's economic position: fuels (mainly petroleum), nonfuel minerals, grains, and other agricultural products (which include tropical beverages and agricultural raw materials of various kinds). These various product groups have experienced very different price movements over the past thirty years or so, with direct and indirect implications for female employment. The price movements of minerals have been of much greater significance to the prospects of entire national economies, to which we turn later in this chapter, than to women directly. It is the developments in grains and other agricultural commodity markets that concern us here, primarily the former.

Nonfood commodity prices have shown enormous price (and to some extent quantity) fluctuations in international markets in the postwar period. This instability has bedeviled periodic attempts by development economists to show that developing countries—so dependent on these products—are inherently disadvantaged by likely movements in the relative prices of the goods they export and import. The price of manufactures has indeed risen steadily in the long term to the disadvantage especially of developing countries whose industrial capacity is small and which therefore have to import their needed supplies of manufactures. But at times, the exporters of agricultural commodities have benefited from very strong upswings in the prices of these products. And though in these markets prices often move conversely to quantities, so that earnings of typical export suppliers change less than prices (or quantities supplied) alone, there have been two periods when prices moved so strongly ahead that real incomes did increase significantly. At the time of the Korean War around 1950, demand for commodities was exceptionally strong and resulted in a surge in commodity prices from 1951 to 1952. Then again, from 1973 onward, inflation and uncertainty in the industrialized countries had the effect of boosting prices of agricultural raw materials and, even more so, tropical beverages relative to other goods. Conditions in the years 1973–78 or 1979 were therefore quite favorable to producers and exporters of these products. But since then, the relative price strength has evaporated, and the value of commodity export earnings has sunk rapidly in relation to the prices of manufactures and minerals.

The most significant price movement fundamentally unfavorable to at least some developing countries' producers has been in the price of grains. There has been a very long-term steady trend of the real price of grains to decline. Price movements in this international market have been much less erratic than for other commodities despite the fact that grains are subject to instability of yields because of changes in weather from one crop year to the next, as with other agricultural crops. This is largely because in wheat, the dominant grain, huge stocks have traditionally been held by the United States, and now also by the EEC, to smooth out the amounts coming into the international market. This dampening device has meant that the grains market has more clearly reflected underlying supply and demand conditions in the largest producing and consuming countries and not so much been disturbed by variations. Demand has risen steadily with great increases in world population over the past forty years, but increases in average yields have led supplies to increase even more strongly. The main suppliers of wheat, corn, and rice to the international market are the industrialized countries, particularly the United States. These countries have achieved dramatic and sustained increases in productivity in grain production in the past forty years. Normal yields are now twice what they were in 1950 (Schuh 1985).

Productivity has also risen, though not to the same extent, in the developing countries, except in Africa. Population growth rates are low in the industrialized countries, and the incremental demand for grains is very small at their high levels of per capital income, so that most of the excess production of grains has gone onto the world market. Even China and India, the two poorest and most populous of developing countries, have improved their yields so much that they have become net exporters of grains—rice and cereals, respectively—in recent years. (These countries nevertheless still have widespread malnutrition—their effective demand is held down by low incomes.) The consequence of this abundance of supplies has been steady falls in world market prices. The real price of wheat was approximately half in the early 1980s of what it was one hundred years before. More recently, in the postwar period, the real price of wheat has declined at an annual rate of 1 percent, the real price of rice by 1.3 percent, and the real price of maize by 2.6 percent between 1970 and 1983 (Schuh 1985). These declines have conferred a very considerable benefit on consumers. Farmers who have kept up with or surpassed the average gains in productivity have maintained their real incomes. But less efficient producers who have not managed—for whatever reason—to increase their productivity have lost out. The divergent performance of different developing countries in this respect has become more pronounced through time and of great significance to the employment of women, who have not been able as producers to capture the gains available.

International Finance

The international financial market has only existed in its present form since the beginning of the 1970s. The United States began to export capital soon after the Second World War, first in aid grants to the European economies and the former Japanese colonies in East Asia, then in the shape of private foreign investment, and then in more widespread aid allocations, for example to Latin America. Investors in the rest of the world were prepared to hold dollars abroad, sustaining the outflow on the United States capital account, because of the dollar's status as effective world reserve currency, based on the huge gold reserves with which the United States emerged from the war (and backed also by the large size of the United States economy compared with others). But these reserves were not inexhaustible, and in 1971 the dollar was unlinked from gold. The fixed price of the dollar in gold terms had been the linchpin of an international system of fixed exchange rates. The establishment of this system was engineered by the Bretton Woods institutions at the end of the war, and its demise essentially made possible the emergence of the private capital market in its present form. A new market was needed in the first instance for the determination of different currency rates (many currencies nevertheless remained tied together in blocs, subgroupings of currencies that retained fixed rates among themselves) and for exchange transactions, but it soon expanded beyond this role into a conduit for flow of finance capital.

A preexisting stock of capital existed in the form of "Eurodollars"—dollars held outside the United States (as counterpart to its capital outflow), which were on-traded by investors in the "Eurodollar market." The currency of some other large industrial countries held abroad came to be added. Two other large sources of funds emerged in the early 1970s. First, from 1971 onward, the United States developed deficits on its current (or trade) account, with the counterpart funds available for on-trading externally. Second, the Organization of Petroleum-Exporting Countries (OPEC)-engineered oil price rises of 1973 and 1979 generated enormous sudden capital surpluses for the oil-exporting developing countries, which were unable to use all their funds for productive local investments and placed them mostly with international banks for on-lending. The private capital market thus became the main channel for the "recycling" of oil revenues.

These various funds underwrote the expansion of private capital markets from the 1970s onward. Three factors led to equivalent growth of demand for funds. First of all, the absorptive capacity of developed (and later developing) countries was larger than their domestic savings: borrowing on the international markets provided funds to bridge the gap and allow countries to fulfil their growth potential more quickly. Second, developing countries increasingly developed deficits on their trading accounts—partly as a counterpart of increased investment, partly with sudden changes in international relative prices in the mid-1970s. Investment required the import of machinery and equipment for new industries, which were too young to generate any foreign exchange earnings themselves through exports (and the industrial investment tended to be carried out behind protective barriers, which undermined exports earnings of other sectors, mainly agriculture, that would lessen the trade gap). Increased growth and prosperity for developing country populations fed demand for consumer imports. And last but not least, the multiple increases in oil prices from 1973 onward suddenly flung the payments of oil-importing developed and developing countries alike out of balance, producing an immediate need for short-term bridging finance.

International capital transactions grew by about twenty percent each year throughout the 1970s, and as in trade in tangibles, developing countries have increasingly participated in this market. By 1980, about sixty percent of capital flow involved developing countries. But the explosive growth of the private capital market has presented major problems to participating countries. The expansion of capital flow in the past has set two requirements for the future. First, the market must continue to expand, to provide finance for extension of outstanding loans on terms tolerable to debtors. Second, to service those loans, debtors must generate foreign exchange earning through sales of goods on international product markets. One or the other of these requirements must be met, or else the system collapses.

The international capital market has emerged without any central authority. The member countries of the International Monetary Fund attempted to fill this role by empowering it to issue Special Drawing Rights (SDRs) as a form of currency not dependent on the performance (and policies) of any single economy. However, in spite of the demands of the developing countries for increased international liquidity, SDRs remain a small item in total flow compared with the dollar. The international capital market has suffered from and remains liable to instability engendered by the fiscal, monetary, and trade policies of particular (large) national economies, particularly the United States. In respect to the two requirements of the system, restrictive monetary policies increase the cost and reduce the availability of funds to the market and threaten its expansion, while restrictive trade policies undercut the ability of debtor countries to repay past loans and thus, by extension, increase their need to borrow more. These generally unfavorable trading terms and high real interest rates are the crux of the current "debt crisis." Crises are supposed by definition to be short-term events, but the term has been used for some years, with justification, to describe the precariousness of the system. In order to understand the genesis and significance of the debt crisis to developing countries—and to female employment in those countries—we have to examine how the international financial and product markets have interacted and been shaped by national policies in the past fifteen years.

The growing international interdependence reflected in the expansion of international exchanges has led to economic growth, but it also implies vulnerability. Economic events in one part of the world can now have widespread international ramifications. The great upheavals that have taken place in the world economy in the past fifteen years have disrupted economic growth and development in many countries that were not the source of the initial difficulties. The industrialized economies are overwhelmingly influential in the world economy, their wealth and income being far greater than those of the rest. Industrialized countries (including the socialist countries of East Europe) account for approximately seventy-five percent of world output as against twenty-four percent of world population. The global problems of the past decade have largely been due to the industrialized countries' internal difficulties, and to the policies they have adopted to deal with them, and with external events in the 1970s, notably the oil price rises. Those external events also affected the developing countries deleteriously, but the measures taken by the industrialized countries have had the more profound and longer lasting impact through their effect on the main parameters of the international economy.

In the past twelve years, there have been two episodes of severe difficulty in 1974–75 and from 1980 onward, respectively. In 1975, economic growth fell sharply in the industrialized countries, from approximately six percent in 1973 to just below zero in 1975. There was a fall from seven percent to under four percent in the same year for developing countries.

The second recession has been worse. It has been both deeper and longer lasting and has affected the developing countries more adversely than before. Industrialized countries' aggregate growth was below 1.3 percent for the four years 1980–83 and was actually negative (−0.5 percent) in 1982. Developing countries' growth fell from an average of over 5 percent from 1973 to 1979 to 2.5 percent from 1980 to 1983 and, according to the latest estimates, to about 3.5 percent in 1984 (World Bank 1984b). Within this total, however, two regions have been badly affected: Africa experienced negative total growth in 1983 while Latin America has had absolute declines since 1981 (World Bank 1984a).

The rises in oil prices were similarly concentrated at two points: 1973–74 and 1978–79. They thus predated the recessions by about two years in each case. The oil price rises were certainly disruptive, but they were not the fundamental cause of the recessions. The industrialized countries were by 1973 *already* experiencing underlying economic problems, and these undermined their capacity to overcome the oil price shock. The experience of Japan testifies to this view. Japan was the industrialized country in principle most vulnerable to the oil price rises because of its almost total dependence on imported energy. But because it has suffered to a lesser extent from the internal problems of the other industrialized countries, it has made the best recovery.

Structural Disequilibria in the Developed Countries

Fundamental imbalances threatening the sustainability of growth in industrialized countries had become entrenched in the course of the 1960s. First, the rate of increase of labor productivity tailed off steadily, but real wages continued to rise faster than productivity. On top of the increasing share wages were taking of national income, there were steady increases in the services provided by the state, above and beyond the revenues generated in taxes. Taken together, these elements

spelled trouble, since they represented overextension of national economic resources. Inflation began rising in the late 1960s, the classical way of accommodating such pressures; it was given a sudden boost by the first oil price rises of 1973–74. At the same time, another factor, unemployment, also began to be apparent as firms shed labor that was increasingly expensive in relation to the value of production. The only benign solution to this set of problems lay in faster capital accumulation and improved productivity growth. But another trend, toward lower corporate profits (which had begun in the early 1960s), deepened, reducing the incentive for companies to invest. The cost of capital was low, with interest rates periodically even negative in relation to inflation; even so, this failed to lead to sufficient investment to improve industrialized countries' economic performance, and rates of economic growth steadily declined.

The second round of oil price rises thus took place when industrialized countries had not only failed to regain fast productivity growth but had seen significant increases in both inflation and unemployment. The policies they then adopted led to the second recession. The reduction of inflation became their main priority. Inflation was indeed brought down relatively quickly in most industrialized economies by restrictive monetary policies, but the deflationary falls in demand that this entailed depressed income and demand in national and international markets. Public expenditure continued to grow beyond tax revenues and, taken in conjunction with the declines in corporate profits (savings), the borrowing requirements of the industrialized countries did not slacken. Moreover, the developing countries' demand for funds rose again while the oil-exporting countries did not at this point have surplus funds available to lend internationally to the same extent as they did after 1973.

This coincidence of strong demand for capital in developed and developing countries alike and the change of monetary policy that led to a tightened supply of funds led interest rates to soar in 1980–81. The burden of servicing the accumulated developing countries' external debt, mostly contracted at adjustable rates and greatly increased after 1973, was greatly magnified. The developing countries' debt increased fivefold between 1974 and 1984; in 1983 it represented about twenty-five percent of their total national income. At the same time, the depressed state of the international product markets made it more difficult for developing countries to sell exports and generate foreign exchange to repay their debts. So was the "debt crisis" born; Latin

America, where most of the debt was concentrated, began a prolonged decline in total income unprecedented for a generation (Molina and Berio 1986).

Some industrial countries, notably the United States, enjoyed something of a recovery in 1984 despite high real interest rates. Developing countries seemed also to be through the worst—growth had gradually picked up since the trough of 1982—though structural conditions remained deeply unfavorable to development. But the cost of the United States' resurgence has been high for the rest of the world, particularly for the developing countries. Given the United States' restrictive monetary policy, the United States' high defense expenditures and public sector borrowing requirements, met by diversion of approximately one tenth of the world's capital flow, are major causes of the continued high level of interest rates. Debtor countries' difficulty is compounded by the high value of the American dollar associated with this capital inflow, as their debt is largely denominated in that currency.

Impact on Regional Development

Many of the Latin American countries are relatively large and have quite high levels of per capita national income. Some of them had achieved considerable income growth in the 1960s and early 1970s on the basis of industrialization aimed primarily at satisfying local markets; they are also mostly (with the exception of Mexico and Venezuela) without energy supplies of their own. Their level of development made them fairly heavy consumers of imported oil, but their industrial sectors were, in general, uncompetitive in international terms. They were thus hit both by oil price rises on the one hand and by the contraction in international trade, in which they were ill placed to expand their export share, on the other. They used the new financial facilities to buy time to adjust to the new international economic environment but were caught by the accumulation of past loans suddenly compounded by the high interest rates of the early 1980s and the high value of the dollar in which most of their loans were denominated. As countries that switched out of import, substituting industrialization, later than the East Asian countries, they were doubly penalized: they missed the boom years of the international product markets in the 1960s, and they fell into the sticky trap of the money markets' lending. Initially it seemed the sweet way to ease the oil shock adjustment, but it soon turned sour. In retrospect, these countries' response to the first oil shock was a costly mistake, but its impact has been magnified out of all proportion by the international repercussions of subsequent industrialized countries' (mainly the United States) domestic policy. The high United States trade deficit has of course had some compensating benefit, since it means that the rest of the world has rapidly increased its exports to the United States—Brazil in particular benefited from this in 1984. But as well as the slightly higher trade restrictions that all developing countries face, it appears that the Latin American countries struggling to increase export earnings and thus their capacity to repay loans have to overcome a second disadvantage: within the set of manufactures exported by developing countries as a whole, those exported by the biggest debtor nations face the highest level of restrictions (Nogues, Olechowski, and Winters 1985).

The sub-Saharan African countries are also in severe economic difficulty. They are much poorer on the average than Latin American countries and their low productive capacity is put even further under stress by the even faster rates of population increase. Their problem lies partly in debt, partly in a currently even weaker potential for earning foreign exchange than the Latin American countries, and partly in dependence on imported food. They are economies with very small industrial sectors and with a corresponding dependence on primary commodities. As the prices of their export goods—cash crops and raw materials—have fallen in the 1980s (without compensating increases in output to boost income), they have been forced to borrow to maintain even minimal levels of consumption for the population. The burden of debt carried by a number of African countries is similar to that of the most indebted Latin American in relation to export earnings and national income. In Africa as in Latin America, therefore, most men and women alike are suffering declines in their standard of living, which is already desperately low. Evidence that women have borne heavier losses in their employment prospects will be examined in later chapters. But it is worth making the point here that in both continents, many women are solely responsible for supporting dependents (i.e., the number of female-headed households is much higher than in Asia) so that families all suffer proportionately; the distribution of income among households has probably worsened.

Asian countries on the whole have been least damaged economically by recession and have been more successful in continuing economic growth during this period, most notably in the continued expansion of export of manufactures. The East Asian NICs, which are the most dynamic economies in the region, export sixty percent of their national output almost entirely in manufactures. They account for almost three quarters of developing countries' total exports of manufactures. Like the Latin American countries, they had borrowed to finance their way through the first oil shock, but the buoyancy of their exports has had the favorable spin-off effect of winning them relatively good borrowing terms so their debt burden was not magnified to the full extent possible by the 1980–81 interest rate increases.

4

Technological Change

International technology transactions have increased greatly over the past forty years. A broad cross-sectoral range of institutions and instruments of transfer now exists, and many new product and process technologies have emerged and been widely diffused internationally, some of them of revolutionary character. While this has made available a great variety of technological options, the criteria governing their choice has, in practice, proved difficult to determine, particularly for the developing countries. Sometimes the attempt to choose, adopt, and adapt technologies that have proved successful in the more developed countries has been accompanied by many problems heretofore unseen. At the same time, the cost of developing "appropriate" technology is far from negligible.

New institutions and instruments of the international market in technology are many and varied, while improvements in communication and information processing have facilitated a greatly accelerated rate of transfer of information.

In agriculture, a set of thirteen new multilaterally funded research institutes (the Consultative Group on International Agricultural Research; CGIAR) has been established around the world whose objective is to promote food production in developing countries. The CGIAR has attracted funds and channeled research efforts to derive new crop varieties and promote improved agronomical methods, make

them universally available, and assist low-income countries in their application. The least developed countries have thus been more fully
drawn into an arena of exchange that already served richer countries
(who have already had access to new agricultural technology on a commercial basis) though the system has not yet compensated for the long-
standing bias against research into crops of special interest to the least
developed countries.

In industry, TNCs have been an important agent of technological
transfer. They have raised the average technological capacity of industry in developing countries by setting up subsidiary operations, in
many cases of superior efficiency to local enterprises. Whether such
operations increase or depress local technological capacity is another
matter. In joint ventures, the transfer is real enough at both managerial
and production levels, but in technologically advanced activities the
production facilities set up are unlikely to meet state of the art standards anyway. For instance, IBM's policy of setting up microelectronics operations only while retaining one hundred percent
control testifies to the reluctance of high-technology enterprises to
share their technology. Otherwise, the extent of transfer is arbitrary
and incomplete, depending on the rotation of staff between the subsidiary and local firms.

TNCs are not the sole suppliers of new industrial technology. There
has been an increasing tendency—in part because of developing governments' pressure—toward the "depackaging" of technology. There
is now a wide range of other instruments of international commercial
transfer: consultancy firms, placement of engineers and other technical
experts, sale and leasing of new and advanced as well as used capital
equipment (the latter sometimes economically efficient at the factor
prices prevailing in developing countries, despite being strictly old
fashioned), licensing of patents, etc.

There have been astronomical improvements in pure and applied
scientific knowledge over the past forty years in many fields. The application and transfer of such innovations internationally depends on
the existence of a technoscientific structure for this purpose.

In agricultural science, massive plant-breeding programs and biological engineering have produced new modern high-yielding varieties
of rice, wheat, and maize. Chemical research and development has led
to new pesticides, weed killers, etc. (though many of these have very
bad side effects when used in uncontrolled conditions and some have
had to be withdrawn from use altogether because they become un-

expectedly counterproductive [e.g., DDT], even when used as intended).

Microelectronics is the other great modern scientific breakthrough with multiple and multiplying applications in industry and services (e.g., communications and information handling). Many new products and production processes have been developed.

The effects of technological change in production processes on labor use in general and on female labor in particular are complex and contentious. Effects on systematic labor use of new *products* are not to be expected. All technological progress increases labor productivity, but otherwise the effects vary with the type of change and the preexisting conditions of employment. For example, a given innovation may lower the level of skill required of a skilled crafts work force but may raise them in a new work force mobilized from rural populations.

Three levels or types of technological change can be distinguished. Improved *tools* accelerate the specialization of labor and raise labor intensity; *mechanization* displaces labor; *automation* increases the degree of engagement and attentiveness required of the work force if not always the necessary level of technical knowledge (Schmitz 1985).

The effects of technological change on female labor specifically are sometimes but not always related to the fact that female labor is cheaper than male. It is a relevant consideration in industry in labor-intensive operations where the only feasible improvements in productivity come from refinements of tools and changes in work flow arrangements and other aspects of production organization. In many "light industries," technological progress has been limited in this way, either because of technical difficulties of mechanization (e.g., in clothing production where the handling of limp materials presents insurmountable problems for machines) or because of the disproportionate cost of capitalizing production operations (as in electronics). As long as production *remains* labor intensive relative to other industries, the incentive is still for employers to minimize labor costs on the one hand and for jobs to remain relatively unrewarding in terms of wages and repetitiveness (i.e., they are "secondary" employment positions) on the other; on both counts, female labor tends to be employed where it is available.

In many light industries, mechanization becomes technically and economically feasible at some point. Some presently quite capital-intensive operations, for example, in parts of the textile industry, were previously highly labor intensive. That technological progress is not steered by economic (labor) cost considerations is clear from the fact that textiles have historically been a very "feminized" industry; economic logic would have directed efforts at labor-displacing technological change toward industries employing more expensive *male* labor.

The "skillfulness" or otherwise of work in labor-intensive operations is often raised in connection with the sex composition of industrial branch work forces. But the notion is conceptually unsatisfactory, and its true relevance to gender a complex matter.

Undoubtedly, the assembly jobs in which women are concentrated in industry do not require many years of training and high-level technical expertise, and in that sense they do warrant their usual description of "unskilled." On the other hand, these are also *not* the characteristics of a great range of other industrial shop floor jobs associated with mechanized operations. The years of training and apprenticeship that male workers in such positions undergo are often more of a historical hangover from the days of polymath craftsmen than a practical necessity in contemporary conditions. (They are retained at least in part as a way of mystifying supposed male skills.) Moreover, the fact that offshore TNCs in Asia allegedly prefer women workers because of their greater dexterity and more extended powers of concentration than men at least suggests that the assembly jobs that are done in these plants need considerable skill in a common sense definition of the term. Nor does work in highly mechanized or in automated plants apparently require much skill in the ordinary sense, since technical advances in this area consist largely in making machines more self-policing, lessening the need for human control and correction. The emphasis on "skill" as the crucial labor characteristic in all situations is misleading, as are attempts to rank jobs in terms of skill and make correlations with the sex composition of the work force—which is usually implicitly done to explain and justify the differences in wages by sex.

In agriculture, by contrast to industry, contemporary changes in process technology are of such a kind that they result in a sex bias in labor use against women. Moreover, *product* technological changes also have a differential effect on labor use by sex, but in this case it is often favorable to women.

Modern high-yielding crop varieties are now recognized to have had a generally employment-creating effect because they raise land productivity so much. Demand for extra labor has *not* been limited to large farms or to unpaid family workers. This incremental employment has been beneficial to women as a means of earning income for two reasons. In countries where general or specific seasonal labor shortages exist, women represent the only major possible source of new labor (because of their current relatively low formal labor force participation rates) that can be mobilized to meet this need. Second, some of the peak labor operations, particularly harvesting, are classed as "women's work" under the usual pattern of sexual division of labor in agriculture.

Modern changes in agricultural process technology are a very different matter. In historical terms, the first-generation technological changes lay in the amplification of power sources available to cultivators (pulleys, gears, animal draft), which, like the invention of the wheel and the introduction of the hoe and later the plough, constituted improvements in tools in economics terms. This type of change has now more or less been completed with refinements to motor power and the widespread provision of electric power (though rural electrification of course has a long way to go).

Agricultural process technology changes are now concentrated on mechanization of different cultivation tasks. The kind of tasks most amenable to mechanization are those with a strongly repetitive "mechanical" character. Men's adoption of previous productivity-enhancing improvements means that the tasks now most subject to mechanism are predominantly carried out by women. In any case, it seems that innovation has historically been more economically induced in agriculture than in industry. The pattern of sexual division of labor, which seems to have existed for as long as records can show, is for women to have primary responsibility for final provisioning of the social group (the household) by way of food preparation and fuel and water collection and for men to concentrate on land clearing and preparation. There is a basis for this allocation of tasks in women's reproductive capacity, which makes them less mobile. Field cultivation tasks are a shared concern but with a certain distinctiveness in the normal contribution of each sex. Male specialization in land preparation extends to ploughing, while women's specialization in the final transformation of food products leads them to be involved rather at the tending (weeding) and harvest and postharvest stages (harvesting itself and threshing and winnowing of grain). These are the very operations that are now proving ripe for mechanization. Hence, all the evidence is that contemporary technological changes in agricultural production processes are not only generally labor displacing (an inherent consequence of mechanization) but specifically squeeze out female employment opportunities.

Technical changes have affected economic activities and the claims on their time in far broader ways than modern economic analysis tends to suggest. The impact varies among, and should be examined at the levels of, the household, the community, and the State (Bryceson 1985).

Technology also affects *forms* of organization of economic production in ways that are relevant to the sexual composition of the work force. Some technologies are more open to "decentralized" production than others—that is, to the use of outworkers away from the controlling premises of an enterprise. Women predominate among outworkers as a whole, most especially among *home*workers, because paid homework is compatible to a degree with the household maintenance work that is women's responsibility. Generally, outwork is possible at the lower end of the technology hierarchy, where efficiency depends on labor specialization based on relatively simple tools. In more mechanized and heavily capitalized operations, the machines tend to be both tightly integrated on site and too expensive to be used by individual workers off the premises. So informal sector outwork, which is greatly underrecorded in official statistics and which international economic factors may well have caused to increase in recent years, takes place in the same types of light industries that employ female labor in the factory sector. It is also possible that the latest wave of innovations based on microelectronics will reverse the tendency of technological change, in its successive stages, to diminish the potentiality for outwork. On both counts, contemporary (and prospective) technological changes may generate more employment specifically for women than has been the experience in the recent past. Technological choice, therefore, whether exercised in enterprises that are public or private, has an immediate impact on women's employment.

Part III

EMPLOYMENT TRENDS
FOR WOMEN BY SECTOR

5

Agriculture

Differences in agriculture and farming systems are ultimately the basis for the differentiation of the economies of whole continents within the developing world. Though oversimplification is an obvious hazard, strong similarities in agricultural practices exist in Latin American countries including Central America and the Caribbean, in African countries with the exception of the North African littoral and Egypt, and Asian countries (though in this case distinctions between South Asia—the Indian South Continent—and the rest and, as a microcosm of the whole, *within* the Indian subcontinent, are fairly pronounced). The "gender dimension" is not a supplementary consequence of variation in agricultural practices but a fundamental organizing principle of labor use, stemming directly from differences in resource endowment and the carrying capacity of the land.

Variations in farming systems and technology are not demonstrated by aggregate employment and labor force data. But statistics on female participation do show the total importance of agriculture in the various regional economies and also where agriculture is more important to women as a source of employment than to men. There are far more women relatively speaking in agriculture in Africa. In 1980, eighty-seven percent of all members of the female labor force in low-income African countries were in this sector, compared with seventy percent of women in India, seventy-four percent in China, sixty-six percent in other low-income Asian countries, and fifty-five percent in middle-income Asian countries. In Latin America, the figure is an extremely low fourteen percent, similar to the significance of agriculture to female employment in developed countries (also fourteen percent for market and centrally planned industrial countries taken together but considerably below that level for Western Europe and the United States [ILO/INSTRAW 1985]).

Participation figures are of course suspect as a guide to the real level of women's involvement in agriculture, however, and official statistics have to be set in the context of ethnographic and detailed labor time use surveys for the information they contain to be properly interpreted. Labor force participation data implicitly use a very narrow definition of agricultural activity, focused on land cultivation, work in the field, and large-scale livestock keeping; the work involved in seed selection, in storing, preserving, and transforming food crops to edible form, and in tending small livestock, for example—all important parts of the full agricultural cycle that tend to be done by women—are often neglected. As a result, the importance of women as a source of labor in agriculture in all regions is much underestimated.

With all those caveats, it is nevertheless clear that conditions in agriculture are overwhelmingly important for African women, of lesser but still marked importance for Asian women, and of little direct relevance nowadays to the bulk of Latin American women. The relative importance of agriculture for female compared with male employment also varies by continent. Women are more important in agriculture than in other sectors in most regions, with the strong exception of Latin America where agriculture is far more important as a source of employment to men than to women. But apart from the last case, the distinctiveness of the agricultural sector by region is not apparent from these comparisons.

The differences in farming systems and technology are based on shortage of good land relative to population in almost all of Asia and on abundance of land in Africa south of the Sahara. In terms of physical ratios, Latin America is close to the African endowment, but the distribution of people to land has been warped by historical and political factors, and for the majority of the population land is in very short supply.

The ratio of land to population is not a constant over time, of course, for several reasons. Growth of population leads eventually to exhaustion of the carrying capacity of the land; population pressure

1986). Modern systems of land registration (again resting ultimately on colonial practice, which held to a benign view of the household as a collectivity with a man as head) perpetuate this tendency. They allocate the land to the men; excluding women from legal title undercuts their ability to raise credit on their own behalf and in that way has far more serious long-term consequences on male and female assets and sources of income than the mere grant of formal title (with use rights in practice undisturbed) would suggest.

The effects of this sexual division of labor on the household are also significant. Women's responsibility for the care and provision of food for members of their household effectively removes men from liability in these matters, should they so wish. Migration of male labor to mines and plantations becomes possible on a permanent and semipermanent basis because women can, by only slight extension of their traditional role, take over the task of family support in its entirety. The system of male migration has developed into a movement of male labor to the towns to search for work in the growing nonagricultural sectors. The search is often in vain, open unemployment being so high, so that the families remaining in the rural areas cannot be sure of receiving cash remittances from their male members. Indeed, on the contrary, the level of open male unemployment means that many unemployed males must be receiving support from their subsistence base back home— behaving, in short, as subsidized "secondary" workers while they seek employment, in a manner usually held as stereotypically female. In the case of women, their dependence within the household is often adduced as part of the explanation of their preparedness to accept *low* wages in employment; in the case of men, such support is held to *raise* the reserve price at which they offer their labor and to bolster male conceptions of a proper wage rate (see the literature on internal migration as reviewed in Berry and Sabot [1978]).

Regardless of the employment success of male migrants to the towns in Africa, the consequence is a high proportion of de facto female-headed households in the countryside. It has been estimated that in Kenya, forty percent of rural households are female headed, in Ghana almost one half, and in parts of Zambia one third (Lele 1986, Pala Okeyo 1985). In southern African countries drained of rural male labor by the movement of male workers to the mines in South Africa, the proportion is probably even higher. This is three or four times the incidence of female-headed households in South and East Asia (though comparable with levels among *urban* populations in Latin America and the Caribbean, for reasons similarly to do with sexually differentiated patterns of labor use in agriculture in that continent, as will be seen).

In Asia, a different pattern of agricultural labor use by sex prevails, in response to the long-standing pressure of population on the land and far more intensive (tool- and material input-using) methods of cultivation. Women's responsibilities, tasks, levels of participation in cultivation, and employment status all differ from the sub-Saharan African norm. Male and female labor contributions tend to complement each other within the production of particular crops, rather than between crops. In this sense, there is less separation of male and female economic spheres. But the organization of crop production is strongly hierarchical in every case, with women definitely having a subsidiary role.

The main similarity of Asia to Africa lies in the prescription that women's special biological role in reproduction extends to care of children and maintenance of the household (*social reproduction,* as it is sometimes called). In agricultural settings, this confers on women a range of quasiagricultural tasks to do with food crop storage and preparation for consumption, care of small livestock (chickens, goats), etc., as well as the often very time-consuming tasks of fuel and water collection.

Apart from this, women's productive role in agriculture in Asia is entirely different from that in Africa, bearing a resemblance rather to patterns of peasant family farming in medieval Europe as described by Boserup (1980). Women work in agriculture, essentially as assistants to men, at certain points in the cultivation cycle. Their specialist contribution to food supplies for the household consists of care of small livestock rather than production of food such as vegetables, even in small plots, and certainly not independent cultivation of food crops as in Africa. Subsistence plots are not important because of the general shortage of land.

Typically, the division of labor by sex gives men the fundamental work of soil preparation. This comprises a set of tasks that become increasingly important with agricultural intensification. Women's labor goes mostly to planting, weeding, and thinning and is used especially at peak times of harvesting both at the harvest itself and in the postharvest grain operations of threshing and winnowing. The total number of operations that women perform is smaller than men undertake.

A major consequence of land shortage in Asia is that large proportions of the national rural populations are either completely landless or own only a plot too small to provide for their own subsistence above poverty level; forty percent of the Indian rural population, for example, is estimated to meet this description. Consequently, there is a large market in labor, the only resource the landless have. There are significant differences in the hiring of male and female workers in this market in terms of seasonal fluctuations in labor use and wage rates. In general, it seems to be the case that the use of female labor is much more seasonal and that female wages are considerably lower than male wages on an hourly basis. The differentiation of tasks by sex clearly contributes to both: the use of female labor on a smaller range of tasks than men which are not spaced evenly through the cycle explains the fluctuations in hiring; and the limitation of total demand that results leads to market-determined wage rates lower for women than for men. Whether or not it can be said that there is a wage differential by sex in the strict sense of unequal pay for identical work (Lipton [1983] for one holds that there is not), there is no doubt that women's earnings are lower over time (yearly and hourly) and that this follows from a strict pattern of sexual division of labor in agriculture.

Participation rates in *wage* labor in Asian agriculture vary with sex, the size of landholding, and family income. Since men control the use of any land owned and have the power to allocate family labor among particular tasks or types of work, it is not surprising to find that rate of participation in wage labor is higher among women than men (Ryan and Ghodake 1984). All wage laborers come from families with relatively small (or zero) amounts of land. Men devote more of their time to their own holdings, and women, as a supplementary source of labor, go to the wage labor market for additional income, to work either on local farms or on plantations (tea, cotton, rubber). The amount of female labor surplus to the requirements of the family holding is indirectly related to the size of the holding. Of course landless men have no choice but to offer all their labor for sale, but the level of labor market participation is less than women's as long as *some* land is held.

Participation in the wage labor market is not the same thing here as formal labor force participation in agricultural activity: the lower rate of total labor force activity among women derives from the fact that above a certain landholding size, women withdraw from the formal labor force as conventionally defined. This is partly a matter of social prestige, especially in cultures where there is a heavy social premium on the seclusion of women, but it partly reflects an increasing (unrecorded) role for women on agriculture and agriculture-related tasks closer to home. With land and asset accretion, there is more work for women to do tending livestock, etc., and less time for outside work. There is a matching correlation, even stronger, between family income levels and the fate of female labor force participation rates; the lower the family income, the higher the rate of female labor force participation, the relationship being much more marked for women than men over almost the entire income range. Below some critical minimum severe poverty income level, female participation does, however, fall off; no doubt such women are discouraged from looking and/or are unable to find work (Lipton 1983).

Much evidence on this and other aspects of labor use in Asian agriculture comes from the Indian subcontinent and should not necessarily be taken to apply to the whole continent. But the pattern nevertheless is consistent with what one would expect of the resource endowment of the region overall—though of course there are countless local variations in social and economic organization and pockets, some large, with atypical endowments relative to population. However, the findings need not be rejected as working generalizations in default of comprehensive data.

For whatever reason, rural to urban migration is not such a prominent feature in Asia as in Africa, and the sex selectivity of migration, though still biased toward males, is far less extreme. In consequence, the incidence of sexually imbalanced households is much lower, and in particular there are far fewer female-headed rural households—on the order of ten to fifteen percent in most Asian societies (Visaria 1980, Lele 1986).

In Latin America, the agricultural sector has become of very slim importance to women as a source of employment, though it was not always so. The effects of colonial penetration were more disruptive of traditional patterns than in Africa, where creeping intensification had begun to reduce demand for male labor and made men available for off-farm wage labor. In the Latin American context, a much greater shift in the female agricultural burden followed from the drawing away of male labor from what had been previously a complementary pattern of sexually divided work (Flora 1985). Women's work load was increased by the need for women alone to provide for the first time for the entire subsistence needs of the family, while at the same time, as in the other regions, they had less access to productive resources, aside from their own labor, in the shape of credit and other inputs and ability to mobilize labor from elsewhere. Under these influences, something similar to the African pattern of labor use among the rural population emerged, with women providing most of the labor for subsistence production and many men engaged in off-farm agricultural and nonagricultural wage employment, mostly in large colonial enterprises of one sort or another.

Economic factors external to the agricultural sector produced even more drastic effects on labor use in the postwar period (Flora 1985). Latin America, in reaction to colonial economic domination, opted for a nationalistic strategy of local industrialization as a means to modernization and higher standards of living. The investment had essentially to come from an agricultural surplus, which had to be generated by increased efficiency in agricultural production. Given the overall low population to land ratio, this meant agricultural intensification based on large-scale mechanization. The land reform movement of the 1960s has to be seen in this light as a policy to enhance efficiency rather than equitable distribution of land, its ostensible purpose. In many countries, concentration of land holdings was scarcely altered after twenty years of reform. This is not inconsistent with the fact that *some* redistribution took place, mostly in the event of poor marginal land; there was at the same time increased consolidation among large holdings at the other end of the scale. Capital for mechanization was subsidized as part of the industrialization program, so that greater economic efficiency was achieved in the larger holdings, which produced the bulk of agricultural output by reducing labor input. The use of labor by sex in agriculture was affected insofar as the reduction in labor demand went along with the ejection of peasant inhabitants of the haciendas (quasifeudal agricultural enterprises, which, until the 1960s, were largely self-sufficient entities with little relation to the outside economy). The subsistence plots that hacienda residents had rented from the landlord were thus no longer available, and the land basis for female subsistence production greatly diminished. Since there was so little total demand for agricultural labor, opportunities for compensating access to wage employment in rural areas were virtually nonexistent for women.

There were two consequences. The rate of female labor force participation in rural areas and the importance of women in the agricultural labor force fell back sharply. Second, the lack of employment opportunities gave many women, probably especially from lower income families, no alternative but to migrate to the cities in search of income. As a consequence, there is strong sex selectivity of migration in Latin America, the reverse of that found in Africa: more women migrate than men, and the sex ratio of urban populations is biased in their direction. But in terms of the sex composition of households, the result is the same: a high incidence of unbalanced families and of children dependent on their mothers for support. There is no logical need of course for this to be the outcome: separation of adult family members increases the share of single-parent (or adult) families, but it *need* not increase the share of multimembered female-headed households compared with male. That this is in fact the universal consequence is merely evidence that women are expected to bear the burden of daily care and sustenance of children by living with them, though the separated father may of course contribute to their *financial* support.

How have changes in international transfers of technology and international trade affected women's participation given these regionally distinct patterns of male and female activity in agriculture? The influences of these two markets have been closely intertwined, while the outcome has been very different from place to place as might be expected in view of the almost polar variations in agricultural production and systems of labor use by sex. It should be noted again that the presentation of trends on a regional basis is only a means of attempting working generalizations on an immensely complex set of events, and there is no pretense that the match of agricultural systems and geographical regions is absolute.

Technological changes in agriculture have taken place both in products and in production processes. The product changes consist of the modern high-yielding varieties of rice, wheat, and corn whose introduction about twenty years ago heralded the "green revolution." After complications with the first introductions (having to do with their greater vulnerability to certain pests and diseases and stress conditions, which offset their average yield increases), successive plant generations have been developed that are in almost every respect an improvement on traditional varieties. They have had the effect of greatly magnifying the carrying capacity of the land where they are grown and contributing in a major way to world increases in grain production over the past two decades.

Production process technological changes introduced in this period do not represent such a discontinuity and leap in capability. But there have been small improvements in implements and in the energy efficiency of powered tools such as tractors, which have steadily reinforced the technical efficiency of agricultural mechanization. Material inputs such as pesticides and fertilizers have also been subject to improvement though in these cases increased availability of supply has probably been more important than qualitative improvements in the products themselves in increasing output in poor countries. Furthermore, the benefit from these inputs is much more equivocal than in the case of high-yielding varieties of plants—though there has been much contention even about the impact of those on rural populations. Many agricultural chemicals have had counterproductive and even seriously damaging effects on soil fertility, on pest resistance, and on human health, which were often unforeseen but sometimes preventable in principle (if not in practice, given the suboptimal methods of application that are normal in the conditions of poor countries).

The net result of combined product and process technological changes in agriculture has been sustained increases in world output of grains considerably above the rate of growth of world population. Normal attainable yields in grain have doubled over the postwar period in the industrialized countries that produce the major part of world grain output (Schuh 1985).

However, the selectivity of these output increases must be noted. They have come mostly from the United States, Europe and Japan, and developing countries in Asia. African productivity has not risen in grains. Moreover, grains are of much less importance in the total range of crops grown in Africa, and agricultural research and development have not so far come up with anything like comparable improvements in crops other than grains. Some of the most important differential consequences for women by region are associated with these limitations in new product technology.

The results of this uneven spread of new product technology in agriculture have been felt in those regions where applications have not been possible through world trade in agricultural, particularly food, products. It is cruelly ironic that it is in the regions where population growth is lowest that increases in food output should have been largest. The excess production of grains from the developed countries has been superfluous to local needs, given that at their high levels of personal income the calorific and nutritional requirements of the population are already met. Extra grains have therefore gone on the world market. In Asia, where population is growing, albeit at a low rate, the food demands are certainly not met in their entirety; as a result, extra production is not available for export in this case (and there would be even less extra production if income distribution and the level of average income were improved sufficiently to allow satiety of local demand for food). Even so, both India and China, the largest countries in the region, have become net exporters of grains in recent years, so that world market supplies of grain have been rising from this region too.

World prices of grains (and by the substitution effect, of other starchy food products) have been falling secularly as a result of increased supplies relative to effective demand. This long-term shift in relative prices of food versus nonfood agricultural products on international markets is one of the most notable developments of the postwar period. It has had ramifications for the costs and scope of national agricultural and food policy, on the incentives for growing the two types of crop, and on the allocation of work and rewards between the sexes.

The impact of these changes on Asian agriculture and on the employment position of women in particular has varied over time and with the prevalence of different types of technological innovation. The effects may be characterized as primary and secondary and have occurred in this sequence in time. The secondary effects are only recently becoming apparent, so further stock can and should be taken of an evolving situation in due course. As far as women are concerned, periodic reevaluation is especially critical, because the specific effects for them seem to be different at the two stages. The primary effect has on balance been favorable to women's employment and economic position, but the secondary one is ominously negative in its implications.

The primary effect has been the direct consequence of the product changes, related to the greatly increased productivity of the land that the changes have ushered in. Land productivity is the determinant of the carrying capacity of the land (resource endowment relative to the population), and as such, increases in yields would in principle be expected to lead to increases in the demand for labor. So it proved in practice, though it took some years for increased demand to be realized, and the total incremental demand for labor was in actuality less fully proportional to increases in output than expected (Lele 1986).

The earliest pessimistic studies of the impact of the green revolution did not come to the conclusion that there would be increased labor demand. In the view of many analysts writing in the later 1970s the high-yielding varieties of crops were having a deleterious effect, especially on the poor: the new varieties were seized on by larger farmers and the distributional effects were thought to be disastrous. The initial benefits *were* probably felt in the first instance by larger farmers, who tend to have better access to extension services and to credit than smaller ones and to be in the vanguard of adopting innovations for these reasons. The pessimism therefore was to some extent justifiable at the time—and also showed a laudable sensitivity to the plight of the poor. But the balance of opinion now is that small farmers and laborers have *not* been discriminated against and have benefited from the new varieties (Lipton 1985). In fact they may have benefited proportionally more, in that there has been an increased use for *hired* labor in relation to family labor, and wage employment is of most benefit to the poor and landless who supply most of the wage labor.

But the secondary effect is not likely to be so benign. The first-round employment benefits may be jeopardized. The increased demand for labor was in fact more than could be met at all times, even by mobilizing all previously economically inactive members of the labor force, and local labor bottlenecks appeared at peak periods, notably at harvest time. This constraint seems to be provoking greater mechanization by farmers, despite the high capital costs (Lipton 1985). The labor displacement that ensues applies not only at the peak but impinges to a greater or lesser extent on the entire cultivation cycle. In a mirror reflection of the employment increase, this decrease will tend to affect hired before family labor, and it therefore has the potential of especially harming the income prospects of the poor.

The ramifications for women of these changes in labor use rest on women's distinctive employment status (i.e., their greater propensity to supply hired labor) and on the specificity of the cultivation tasks they carry out. The implication of the first-round changes, which increased the use of labor, especially hired labor, was that employment prospects for women were relatively improved by the introduction of high-yielding varieties of crops. In India, for example, where the total increase in output attributable to the new varieties was considerable, there was a significant rise in the female labor force participation rate in rural areas between 1972–73 and 1977–78 (Krishnamurty 1985) probably stimulated by the increased demand for agricultural labor in this period; in fact, the rate of female unemployment is also estimated to have risen, but it remained very low (at two percent at the end of the period), and almost all the incremental female labor force was absorbed.

Agricultural mechanization is generally acknowledged to displace female labor more than male (Sen 1985, Pala Okeyo 1985). This is a direct consequence of the sexual division of labor, which confers the sorts of small-scale, repetitive "mechanical" jobs such as weeding and

harvesting on women. As the adjective *mechanical* suggests, these operations prove particularly amenable to mechanization. The stage of technological development that seems to have been reached in agriculture has superseded the mere refinement of tools, which can enhance the labor intensity of production and consists of replacing human hands with mechanical arms or procedures. The high capital cost of many such innovations is no longer a disincentive to farmers when the alternative is an absolute shortage of labor at critical periods. Many of the tasks at harvest, the main seasonal peak, are done exclusively by women (whose own seasonable participation in wage labor is at its highest at this point). Mechanization directed at superseding labor shortages at the harvesting peak, in combination with the greater general susceptibility of female labor to displacement means that this secondary impact of the high-yielding varieties looks doubly set to undermine women's employment prospects.

Thus, the balance may be tipping, after an initial advantage, *against* women in Asian agriculture. This is an effect on women as producers in the field (albeit as wage labor, rather than as landholders). There is an undoubted consumption benefit to them from reduced grain prices, as to all members of the population, especially the poor whose diet contains a proportionally large amount of staple grains. But contrary to usual opinion, women do not, according to an authoritative recent review, constitute a disproportionate share of low-income groups—with the very major qualification, however, that they *are* unduly heavily represented among the lowest few percentiles of the population as opposed to the several deciles falling below the poverty line, i.e., they are heavily represented among the ultrapoorest (Lipton 1985). Thus, with the exception of that critically vulnerable group, women cannot fall back on their consumption laurels, as it were: as in all other sectors, their economic position depends most importantly on their employment prospects. This is true even more for them than for men in agriculture, because women lack access (relatively, if not always absolutely) to other income-generating resources and have only their labor to sell.

The main ill effect of the introduction of modern high-yielding crops in Asia has been on those *not* able to grow them (Lipton 1985). The yield increases have been so great that marketed supplies have increased significantly and brought grain prices down, to the detriment of farmers growing the same or competing crops in climatically different areas. Failing to achieve increases in output themselves, their income falls proportionally. The same thing has been happening at the regional level. Africa's miserable agricultural state cannot be seen in isolation from what has been happening elsewhere in the world. The impact of technology on African agriculture has been felt indirectly through its contribution in raising Asian (and North American, European, and Japanese) agricultural productivity and bringing down food prices on international markets.

Since there is in general a strong pattern of specialization by crop by men and women agriculturalists in sub-Saharan Africa, with women responsible for food crops, it follows that male and female income and employment benefits are directly related to the prices of their respective products. Between 1970 and 1983, the real world price of wheat declined at an annual rate of 1 percent, rice by 1.3 percent, and maize by 2.6 percent (Schuh 1985). By analogy again with the distribution of benefits in Asian agriculture, these prices should at least have brought a benefit to the poorest people in Africa as consumers. But this does not universally follow. It is true enough for urban populations but not for rural ones. Land scarcity and therefore landlessness are not (as yet) a general problem in Africa, and the nonagricultural sectors are very small in the rural areas, so food is primarily the source of income and the basis of purchasing power for the rural poor, rather than an item to be puchased from income gained in other ways.

World prices of tropical nonfood crops grown in Africa have fluctuated tremendously in the postwar period. The prospects of these people whose incomes derive from these products has accordingly been very unstable over time and not in any sense the direct converse of those incomes based on food crops. (The picture is complicated, however, by normally compensating fluctuations in output, which do a great deal to stabilize incomes for the *average* producer). There have been two periods of very high prices, one around 1950, the time of the Korean War, and the other in the late 1970s when inflation in the developed countries increased import demand and fueled speculative commodity purchases. Since 1980, however, the prices of coffee, cocoa, and the like have virtually collapsed on international markets.

The price paths of food and nonfood commodities have had their impact on producers in individual countries mediated by local price and investment policies in the agricultural sector. Producer incentives have been improved on the whole for production of nonfood cash crops (with some notable exceptions, such as the persistent holding down of the cocoa price in Ghana) and have been decreased for food crops in a misguided attempt on the part of governments to improve living standards for the poor. Compounding the imbalance, such investment and research and development as has taken place locally has been concentrated on the cash crop sector and traditional food crops have been entirely neglected. International agricultural research efforts have so far failed to compensate, as no progress has been made in developing new tropical foodstuff varieties.

The implications of these developments for women are depressingly obvious. African food producers *are* women. The fact is not irrelevant, of course, in explaining the chronic lack of interest of governments in this sector to date. Even apart from the absence of new varieties of crops—which is certainly in part due to inherent scientific difficulties in devising new plants for African soil and climatic conditions—other ways of increasing output were not applied. For example, increased application of fertilizers and better irrigation could have raised yields on traditional crops, but they were not available to women, who lacked access to credit to purchase such inputs or political leverage to press for infrastructural improvements. Agricultural changes instead took the form—in an attempt to maintain food availability for a growing population—of ever greater exploitation of the land by existing labor-intensive methods. The process was not sustainable in the long run and has begun to result in massive environmental degradation of vast tracts of territory south of the Sahara. Women and children, as the bulk of the rural population, form the majority of the millions of environmental refugees who have had to flee the land as a result. The only resource women have had available to themselves was to produce more child labor, in the shape of more children to help in agricultural production. But this individual rationality has had the sad effect of worsening the problem still further, increasing population growth rates far above the feasible carrying capacity of the land. The poverty and dependence on agriculture of the whole region make it almost impossibly difficult for any surplus to be generated locally for investment in more productive activities outside agriculture, and external credit is used up with imports of food to feed the people.

There are some indications that as well as the impoverishment to which African women, along with all other members of the population of the region, are subject, their relatively strong economic position vis-à-vis men in their societies, based on traditional use rights in land and autonomy in some production activities, may be undermined by another consequence of the deterioration of the land resource base. Land *shortages* are emerging for the first time in parts of the region—for instance, Kenya. This change in the relative resource endowment is one that will, if principle and practice elsewhere are any guide, disadvantage women and prejudice their access to land and complementary inputs in the future, via the tendency for formalization of land titles to be done in men's names. Much research effort at the international level is finally being done relative to improving means of food production in this region, and the essential role of women is at last being recognized in this context. Should new varieties of tropical foodstuffs be successfully introduced, then the disadvantages for women of recent international changes in this region ought to be redressed. But women will not be in a position to adopt the new varieties and benefit from increased productivity and incomes if, meanwhile, a tendency sets in to deprive them of returns for their labor and, indeed, access to land and credit.

6

Industry

Since 1950, the proportion of adult women joining the labor force has risen in both developed and developing countries, though much more markedly in the former. It is difficult to ascribe to international factors any specific contributory role in this. But the international economy *has* led to an increase in the female labor force in one area: it has caused a relative increase in the employment of women in the manufacturing sector in developing countries.

In all developing countries, employment has been growing faster in industry and services than in agriculture. The sectoral distribution of the female labor force has been shifting in accordance with this pattern, moving into industry distinctly faster than the *male* labor force. As a result, the proportion of women in the industrial labor force in developing countries has been rising, from 21 percent in 1960 to 26.5 percent in 1980. The increase took place while the overall share of women in the total labor force remained constant at around thirty-two percent. There are now several individual developing countries where women are more important in the industrial labor force than they are in any developed country. In Hong Kong, South Korea, Taiwan, the Philippines, Singapore, Thailand, Tunisia, and Haiti, for instance, the share of women in the manufacturing labor force is more than forty percent—in Hong Kong, Taiwan, and Tunisia it is approximately fifty percent—while in no industrialized market economy do women account for more than thirty-one percent. On average within each region, women are more important in the industrial labor force in developed countries (where they are 29 percent of the total compared with 26.5 percent in developing countries); however, taking into account that there are fewer women overall recorded in the total labor force in developing countries (thirty-three percent compared with forty percent in developed countries) it can be said that women are less *underrepresented* in industry in the developing countries. But even so, the share of women in the industrial labor force of less developed countries (LDCs) is still lower than their share in the overall labor force (twenty-six percent versus thirty-two percent).

The increasing importance of women in the industrial labor force in developing countries has been systematically related to international factors in two ways. First of all, the rate of mobilization of female labor into industry has been fastest where the rate of growth of total industrial output and employment has been the most rapid. In the period we are concerned with, the most rapid total industrial growth has taken place in countries that have most integrated their industrial sector with the international market, that is to say, that have increased their exports of manufactures at the fastest rate. It follows from this three-way association among rates of industrial growth, export orientation, and increasing female employment that the latter two factors have been correlated with each other as well as with industrial growth per se.

But there is also a direct link. The sexual division of labor takes a very pronounced form in industry in terms of the distribution of male and female workers by industrial branch. Women are typically concentrated in branches making light industrial consumer goods by relatively labor-intensive techniques. (In many countries, even industries of this kind do not use female labor; however, the reverse situation of women employed in heavy, capital-intensive production is never found.) These light industries are mostly of a traditional kind, but they have a new strategic value to developing countries in the modern world economy. What this means is that exports of manufactures from developing countries have been made up in the main of the kinds of goods normally produced by female labor: industrialization in the postwar period has been as much *female* led as *export* led. The very rapid growth of manufactured exports from developing countries has therefore led to a specific demand for female labor and relatively fast growth of female employment in industry. In terms of the level of female employment then, the influence of the international economy has been more clearly favorable in industry than in any other sector at this aggregate level. But the assessment gets complicated when the distribution of employment creation and the conditions of work are considered: in particular, the international factor has also put a premium on low wages. The benefits are thus highly equivocal.

Nevertheless, on balance, these events have been good for women. There is an absolute gain for women in earning cash, as opposed to working without any monetary reward. In an exchange economy, to be without the means of exchange is truly to be powerless. By implication, the conditions of work undertaken must be a secondary consideration, however deplorable they are. The only exception to this ranking is if the conditions of earning cash are such that they seem to preclude any consolidation of women's position in the cash economy. This would be either because the work is so temporary that expectations are not affected by it or because women have no control over their earnings *and* the work is not acknowledged as productive for some reason, despite money usually being seen as a flag of acknowledgment in this respect. These considerations are relevant to conditions of work for women in the electronics industry and in domestic outwork, respectively.

But first it is important to be clear about the relation between the sexual division of labor in industry and the various dimensions in which the international economy impinges on the sector. There is a more subtle process at work than is suggested by the statements that, on the one hand, the sexual division of labor in industry is such and such, and, on the other, the international market has provided an effective source of extra demand for the products of female labor. There are two modifications to be made. First, there is an integral connection between the existence of female labor in certain parts of industry and the deepening of international integration in manufactures: it is not that the *products* of female labor have gained market share internationally but that female labor per se has been the basis of international competitiveness. Second, it is not the case that the sexual division of labor is a given fact of industrial economic life. There are similarities in the disposition of female labor by branch across countries, as well as certain underlying tendencies that have an economic rationale to them, but the actual *pattern* of distribution by branch varies from time to time under certain influences.

The international market is one such influence; it has probably been working to *consolidate* the concentration of women workers in some particular sectors of industry, thus intensifying rather than just drawing on fixed patterns of sexual differentiation. Therefore, the term *women's jobs* is not used in this context, since it has the connotation of a permanent set of jobs given only to women. The jobs women do, to be sure, have distinctive characteristics, but the jobs themselves vary according to circumstances.

The distribution of the female labor force in industry does not always cover the same set of activities—nor is there a set of activities (except perhaps two to which we return shortly) of which a larger or smaller number is always carried out by female labor, according to the size of the female labor force in industry. But there *is* undoubtedly always concentration of female labor within the industrial sector (there is also, of course, an uneven distribution of male workers in industry; however, unlike female workers, male workers cannot be said to be crowded into a small subset of the whole range of activities).

The industries in which female labor is found can be characterized as light industries, producing consumer goods of varying degrees of modernity, ranging from food processing, textiles, and garments to chemicals, rubber and plastics, and electronics. Concentration or crowding is measured by comparing the proportional importance of women workers in a particular industry with their share in the industrial labor force as a whole. In these terms, crop processing (tobacco mostly) is a heavily female industry in India, employing three times as many women as there are in the industrial sector as a whole (thirty-three percent as opposed to ten percent); in South Korea, textiles is a feminized branch, employing closer to twice the overall share (sixty-seven percent as opposed to forty-three percent); in Hong Kong, India, South Korea, the Philippines, and Kenya, clothing is feminized, with around twice the overall share of female labor on average; in Kenya and Egypt, chemicals production is feminized to about the same degree; rubber employs a disproportionate share in Hong Kong, South Korea, and Egypt, as does plastics in Egypt; and electricals (mainly electronics) is heavily feminized in Hong Kong, South Korea, and the Philippines, among other countries. In these six countries, those seven industries together employ between seventy-five and ninety-four percent of the total female industrial labor force, compared with between forty-four and sixty-five percent of the male (ILO 1984).

Clothing and electronics are the two industries that almost universally employ disproportionately large numbers of women. In other cases, the industries concerned often use disproportionately *few* women; the food processing industry is a case in point and in Hong Kong and the Philippines uses only about half the proportion of women found in the industrial labor force overall. These industries all display a common economic characteristic: they are relatively labor-intensive in their production methods. Not all labor-intensive industries employ women, but all female-employing industries are labor intensive.

Women workers are also bunched in terms of the *occupations* they carry out. While it is not possible to talk of a hierarchy of industries as such (as there are as many possible rankings of industries in different dimensions), there is a standard occupational hierarchy of jobs classified by skill levels and promotional prospects. Women tend to be placed in jobs that are inferior in these terms, doing repetitive, short-cycle, relatively quickly learned tasks for which thorough technical knowledge of the production process as a whole is unnecessary; assembly line work is stereotypical. These jobs are categorized as unskilled. Women are concentrated the world over in unskilled jobs of this kind. It has been shown, for example, that in France women perform more assembly line and machine-paced work and that, even when they are classified as skilled workers, they are more likely to be doing piecework and repetitive operations than unskilled and semiskilled male workers (Kergoat, cited in Humphrey 1984).

Women tend also to be placed in what are sometimes called *dead-end jobs*, that is, jobs from which there are no promotion lines leading on to more varied and rewarding work within the enterprise—work that would entail training to higher levels of complexity and that would be seen as more responsible and accordingly better paid. In industries with mixed work forces, even heavily feminized ones, there is a tendency for the men who work alongside women in end-of-the-line production jobs to take these jobs only in the expectation of getting promoted up to supervisory positions. Men monopolize such upward chains as exist (often, of course, being recruited initially at higher levels of command than women ever achieve). Within manufacturing industries, in other words, women are crowded into the bottom of the command pyramid, without formal responsibility for production, with no decision-making capability within the terms of the enterprise. There is an obvious analogy with the situation in agriculture and also in the services sector in this respect.

Why are women concentrated in work of this kind? It is not easy to separate women's labor market characteristics from the features imposed on their behavior by the type of work they do, but it is not impossible. There are three distinct dimensions of differentiations between male and female labor, relating to wages, education and training, and degrees of deference.

First, women's earnings are lower than men's. In 1982, the ratio of female to male earnings in manufacturing averaged seventy percent for the eight developing countries for which information was available (and sixty-nine percent in seventeen developed countries) (ILO/INSTRAW 1985). This is partly a consequence of the occupational distribution, with women being more important in low-grade occupations. But it is increasingly recognized that women's earnings are less than men's even in the same occupation and for the same job (Lele 1986; Treiman and Roos 1983; Lloyd and Niemi 1979). This wage differential is reduced but not eliminated by adjusting for differences in educational attainment and training between male and female workers.

The main correlates of men's higher wages seem to be seniority and work continuity. At the macroeconomic level, that is, there are no factors apart from men's longer and more continuous time in employment that can explain by association why the differential exists. (Women's absences for childbearing and child care reduce their total time in wage employment.) But microstudies of manufacturing employment suggest that employment practices that make sense only as instances of gender discrimination are the real cause. It has also been established in another context that interpersonal status plays a major part in determining wage differentials among workers within the firm (Frank 1984).

A few of the small number of case studies on employment practices illustrate the kinds of discriminatory treatment in existence. A study of Brazilian firms examined why educated women who were carefully selected and trained for several months on the job were paid less than male workers for whom recruitment was virtually unconditional and no entry qualifications and no training were required (Humphrey 1985). Another showed that in one large organization, women were consistently placed in jobs in the lower points of the grades to which their qualifications and experiences entitled them (Malkiel and Malkiel 1973). A third, econometric study showed that in one country (Taiwan), across manufacturing as a whole there was something akin to what might be called a "marital masculinity premium" as an element in wage determination. Workers' marital status had a definite influence on wages, but for males it was a positive increment, for females a negative one (Gannicott, 1986). Marriage *may* lead to productivity-related differences; for instance, women's absentee rate may rise on marriage, while married men's attendance and reliability are enhanced, but it is extremely unlikely that differences in absentee rates are proportional to the wage differential. In any case, what little concrete information is available on labor turnover and absenteeism by sex (Humphrey 1985, Joekes 1985) shows no such systematic difference and furthermore often shows that female absentee rates are *lower* than men's. The prevailing wisdom that women's absentee rates are higher probably derives less from reality than from the ideological stereotype of the female role, which requires women to give their families first claim on their time, over and above the demands of their job.

The male wage premium in Taiwan is a clear expression of the "breadwinner" ethic—the apparently universal idea that men are responsible for the material support of familial dependents. This idea encapsulates the concept of women as "secondary" workers, uninterested in promotional prospects in employment and satisfied to bring home a mere supplementary income to the household. This idea is enormously powerful in reinforcing sexual stratification, and it legitimizes women's inferior treatment in industrial work in both men's and women's eyes. It accounts for the fact that neither men nor women are in general concerned to press for equal rewards for equal work between workers of different sex. The fact that vast numbers of *women* are in practice responsible for the upkeep of dependent children, and that even in multiple-income households women's incomes are usually devoted solely to household expenses (unlike male earnings) and thus contribute as much or more to household maintenance and reproduction than men's, does not disturb the ideology of gender relations in this respect. As long as only the minority of women support their families on their own, however (even if that minority is forty-nine percent), some theorists claim on grounds of statistical probability that this is a justifiable reason to pay women less, whatever the injustice in individual cases.

There are undoubtedly *some* women whose concern for equitable return for their labor is weak because it is not their only (or main) means of support, so they do not bargain hard on wages. Then there are others who *are* desperate for work, being breadwinners themselves in the conventional sense and solely responsible for the support of themselves and others. They have to accept the low wage set because it is tolerated by the first group; sometimes they even have to take less money if they are considered "unfeminine" workers, likely to be troublesome because they are more determined to get a fair deal for themselves.

The second dimension of sex differentiation in labor markets is that women tend to be less educated than men, according to the normal bias in educational provision in favor of males. There seems little doubt that there *are* significant differences by sex in the labor force regarding both school educational preparation (World Bank 1984a) and vocational training and that women have fewer skills in this sense. But again, microstudies put into question whether the differences are large enough fully to explain the distribution of male and female labor by occupational level. Job descriptions in terms of skill level are normally closely matched to wages, and this is taken to mean that higher skills are rewarded by higher wages. But the match can be interpreted differently. The *wage* level attached to a job may set its skill label in a purely nominal sense (Phillips and Taylor 1980). The Brazilian study cited above (Humphrey 1985) provides examples where the real skill levels of "female" jobs are clearly higher than those of more highly paid male jobs, despite the fact that the official job gradings denote them as lower skilled in accordance with the ranking by wages.

All such apparently anomalous cases can be explained by reference to the prior existence of different wage rates by sex. Differing male and female wage rates are the product of market forces in segmented labor market conditions resting on discriminatory social gender relations, such as are reflected in the "breadwinner" ethic. Discrepancies between skill levels and wages in women's jobs compared with men's can be explained as a consequence of the employers' being able to pay women the going female wage rate and *then* determining the nominal (as opposed to real) skill level of the job in conformity with that lower wage. It is not clear to what extent occupational descriptions would be altered if real rather than nominal skill levels (in this sense) were to be recorded. But this consideration does nevertheless point back to a truly discriminatory element in the observed differential in male and female wages.

Third, there is another attribute that differs between male and female workers, though it cannot be quantified like the first two. This is the degree of deference to command—obviously a useful attribute to the employer in ensuring lack of protest to orders and general cooperativeness in the business of production. In anecdotal accounts of employers' preferences for female labor in certain industries, women's greater "docility" and their "nimble fingers" are the kinds of reasons given by employers themselves. More measurably, it seems to be the case universally that women are less likely to take up membership of a trade union. In the industrial context, labor organizations are of course an instrument of protest as well as of collective bargaining. It is clearly part of the definition of femininity in most if not all cultures that women should be modest, self-effacing, and deferential to their superiors to a greater extent than men; in society, women have a great many more superiors to defer to than men do, in accordance with their inferiority in all the dimensions we have already discussed—in wealth and access to resources, in returns to their labor, and in decision-making powers.

These three dimensions of differentiation of male and female labor, set against the characteristics of production in light industry, explain the concentration of women in this area. First, light industrial consumer goods production tends to be relatively labor intensive. For a given work force, capital goods production uses a larger complement of machinery and equipment and higher valued materials and components. It is not surprising in this perspective that the industrialized countries, with their greater accumulated wealth, should have relatively large capital goods sectors; and it is also in the broadest sense congruent with the developing countries' relative lack of capital and abundance of labor that light industries have greater weight in the structure of their manufacturing industry.

The relevance of labor intensity of production to the sex composition of the labor force is twofold. First, since wages are proportionally much more important than capital as a factor in costs of production in labor-intensive industries, in competitive markets light industrial firms must minimize their unit labor costs as a priority. This can be done by enhancing productivity and/or paying lower wages. Employers' scope for enhancing productivity in these industries is on the whole limited to training and organizational and work flow improvements rather than to radical changes in machining methods and tool design. Although significant savings can be made in these ways, the imperative to minimize wages remains overwhelming. The option of using cheap female labor is an obvious solution to this problem. The greater docility and obedience of female than male labor in this perspective not only strengthens the unit labor cost advantage of female labor but adds to the potential for successful organizational changes in production procedures, which rest on the cooperation of the work force.

Second, in light consumer industries, one of the restrictions in the use of female labor met with elsewhere is no hindrance to the employment of women (Armstrong 1982). This is the prohibition on night shift work by women, which is often enshrined in social custom and is also found on the statute books of most countries. For heavy industrial firms using continuous processes, frequent shutdowns are prohibitively expensive for technical as well as financial reasons. Continuous round-the-clock working is the norm, and a proportion of the work force works at night. In other capital-intensive operations, there need not be technical reasons but there is a purely economic incentive to continuous working. Expensive equipment needs to be worked as much as possible to defray the fixed cost it represents. In lightly capitalized industries, by contrast, the value of equipment is small relative to the cost of labor. Operations can afford to be rested overnight, especially in view of the labor premiums that usually have to be paid for night work. In these industries, therefore, with no pressures on producers to operate at night, employers can and do employ all-female work forces without coming up against the social and legislative barriers against women working at night.

The wage differential by sex and two aspects of women's social role (docility and lesser mobility) are thus directly relevant to the requirements and conditions of labor-intensive production. So also are women's lesser education and training, along with their aforementioned deference or docility, in respect not so much to the economic characteristics of production in this type of enterprise but to the type of work that is generated for employees. Women's docility is also highly relevant when it comes to the stability, or otherwise, of employment, which has become a more important question in the past few years with the recessions in the world economy.

Labor-intensive production tends to generate repetitive tasks for the work force. Primary mechanization of the type used in industry increases the specialization of labor by refining and subdividing tasks into their component parts among different workers, whose job is to achieve speed and accuracy in narrowly defined operations. Jobs of this kind are conventionally classed as unskilled, on the basis that they are quickly learned and no special qualifications or knowledge of the wider production operation is required of the workers. Assembly line work is the ultimate expression of the subdivision and refinement of manual tasks. The work entailed *may* be unskilled in a real sense or, as in the Brazilian case, may clearly require such high performance and need such long preparatory training for select recruits that the description is a clear misnomer. In either case, the work is of its nature extremely monotonous. It is also true that each operator has a crucial role in the production chain, despite the particular task being such a small part of the whole. Production is so integrated that a breakdown in one link cripples the whole exercise. The worker is thus in a position of considerable power over the progress of production, despite the lack of formal authority in production decisions.

Women's lesser education and their expectations (born of past experience) of receiving little training make them apparently suited to unskilled occupations and, most importantly, prepared to stay at such unskilled jobs, however monotonous they may be. Their docility, moreover, makes them unwilling to explore the power they have in the production process. Also, in terms of the command structure of a productive enterprise, there is a strong logic in putting those amenable to orders at the bottom of the ladder.

The process of increased specialization of labor through simple mechanization is not to be confused with the changes in work requirements brought about by technological change in the fullest sense. (Of course mechanization is a form of technological progress in so far as it improves labor productivity, but it usually does little to reduce labor intensity.) Automation and other applications of scientific advance to industrial processes are usually associated with increased capital intensity on the one hand and "masculinization" of the work force on the other. Changes in the textile industry are a good illustration. As textiles has been automated, women workers have been displaced, falling in Colombia, to take the best documented case, from seventy-four percent of the total workforce in 1938 to thirty-two percent in 1979 (UNIDO 1984). It is possible that similar variations in techniques of production in given industries in different countries can also be explained in these terms. For example, as we have seen among the six developing countries for which labor force branch distribution data are available by sex, food processing was heavily feminized only in India; in Hong Kong, the Philippines, and South Korea, women are underrepresented in this branch. The obvious difference between the two sets of countries is that India is much poorer, and the food processing industry (mostly in this case tobacco production) is far less capitalized.

The explanation amounts to what might be called a social theory of male cartelization. Men work in occupations where technological change leads to such increases in labor productivity that employers can pay higher wages. "Male" jobs are characterized as more skilled to lend justification to the higher wages that men demand and can obtain in such circumstances (Cockburn 1981). However, productivity changes are the result not only of factor costs but also of final product prices, themselves determined in part by market conditions. Final prices and thus labor productivity are higher, other things being equal, the more uncompetitive the market conditions. The potential for male claims is contingent on market conditions and the labor supply situation; competitive forces are an influence on the distribution of employment between men and women. Competition acts against male advantage. The significance of increased international integration in developing countries in this context is that it has increased the degree of competition to which industry is subject. The reason why it has not acted similarly in developed countries—which have also, as we have seen, increased their exports of manufactures considerably in the postwar period—is that differences of endowment have conferred a comparative advantage in labor-intensive products on developing countries, while conferring an advantage in capital-intensive ones (and therefore a decreased output of labor-intensive goods, also employing women) on developed countries. In the latter countries, the proportional importance of women in the industrial labor force has been declining steadily—at an increasing pace as a consequence of the recessions.

Competition undermines male claims on jobs in two ways. First, competition among producers keeps final product prices down, depressing labor productivity and lowering potential wages. Garments, plastics, food processing, and other such cheap product industries characterized by large numbers of local producers are examples of this effect. One case is documented where the proportionate use of female labor, even in these usually already feminized industries, was increased further as exports rose—that is, as the industry became more competitive internationally (Joekes 1982a). The firms concerned acted to reduce costs in response to competitive pressure rather than in response to the increased availability of female labor or other such possible considerations. Also, even in industries that are in aggregate highly capital intensive, the strength of competition can drive firms to minimize labor costs in those parts of production that are labor intensive, making savings, in other words, wherever they can. The prime example here is the electronics industry, which has always been extremely competitive at the global level and where, as we have seen, certain separable segments of the production process are labor intensive. (There must be similar separable labor-intensive operations in other branches too, where total costs could also be reduced by global sourcing but where the industry is oligopolistic and profit maximization does not depend strictly on cost minimization.)

In this perspective, the availability of cheap female labor has been crucial to the rapid growth of developing countries' manufactured exports. The product composition of these exports bears out this interpretation: it is weighted toward labor-intensive products made by female labor. Female labor is even more important in the export sector of developing countries' industry than in the industrial sector as a whole.

The main feature is the predominant weight of textiles, clothing, and footwear. These items accounted for thirty-seven percent of developing country manufacture exports in 1975, though by 1981 the share had fallen to twenty-six percent. The drop was due to the diversification of middle-income developing countries, which in that year derived about one quarter (twenty-three percent) of their export earnings from these goods; however, exports remained of major importance to low-income countries, where they contributed fully forty-two percent of earnings from manufactured exports (World Bank 1984a). Other major products exported are electronics components and consumer goods, which accounted for about six percent of total manufactures exports in the early 1980s; a miscellaneous set of other items comprising such consumer goods as sports goods, plastic wares, toys, leather goods, and so on account for the bulk of the remainder. Of the main female-employing industries, only food processing is not a major exporting activity, though some countries are exceptional in this respect (Morocco, for example, where canned fish and vegetables and fruit are important).

The East Asian NICs have been expanding their exports of higher technology products following the Japanese example of economic growth (Scott 1985). But even so, the process is still in its infancy; despite these trends, the NICs *are* still heavily dependent on the usual developing country export goods, particularly textiles and garments. In South Korea and Hong Kong, textiles and garments account for thirty-three and thirty-four percent, respectively, of manufactured exports (in Singapore the share is less) (World Bank 1984a).

The growth of female employment in industry in developing countries is associated with three separate indices, and these themselves are closely correlated. It has been highest in the countries with the fastest rates of overall economic growth and industrial growth in particular; in those countries that together are commonly known as the NICs; and in Asia where, as we have seen, most of the NICs are found (but not all, which gives scope for examining what has happened in the *non*-Asian

NICs, giving some sort of check on the hypothesis of the importance of the influence of international competitiveness on the demand for female labor).

The three main continental regions of the developing world have as a stylized characterization taken distinctive economic paths as a result of the world recessions; differences in performance have been closely related to the degree of international competitiveness in international product markets. Hence, it is not surprising to find that the pattern of female employment in industry also falls into regionally distinct shape. Female industrial employment has in fact grown absolutely in all three continental regions, in accordance with the general increase in population and spread of industrial capacity throughout the developing world. But it has grown fastest in Asia and slowest in Latin America. The female industrial labor force increased by fifty-six percent in the developing countries on average between 1970 and 1980 and by sixty-two percent in middle-income Asian countries, fifty-six percent in middle-income African countries, and only forty-three percent in middle-income Latin America. The differences do not seem very large, but they are more pronounced set against the local rates of population increase: population increased *slowest* in Asia but considerably faster in Latin America and Africa, inversely to the pattern of female industrial employment growth.

There has been a strong association between rate of growth of female industrial employment in the regions and growth of manufactured exports—not just general economic growth. The exploitation of export markets gives access to markets that are (in principle) infinitely larger for any one country, permitting relatively fast expansion of total industrial capacity. Part of the reason for the strong growth of female employment in industry in Asia lies in the strong general growth in demand for all industrial labor in this continent, which cannot be met by male labor alone: women have to some extent got drawn into employment in industry residually to increase total labor supply. (They also get expelled from the labor force when there is any reversal.) But the occupational segregation of the industrial labor market by sex allows a direct connection to be made between export performance and female employment. Increases in exports translate into specific demands for female labor because manufactured exports mostly consist of the types of goods produced by female labor, as discussed earlier. Moreover, international markets are inherently competitive. In so far as labor costs are a major element in production costs, which they are in the industries where women are concentrated, competition tends to drive employers to cheapen the costs of labor. Since women are the source of the cheapest labor, increasing export orientation tends not only to favor the light industrial consumer products in which developing countries have a comparative advantage over others but also to increase the use of female labor *within* such industries. (Most such industries, though "feminized," still use a certain proportion of male labor.)

The association between female industrial employment growth and manufactured exports holds both over time and across individual countries. First, the importance of women in industrial employment in the developing countries increased faster in the 1960s than in the 1970s, as did the rate of growth of developing countries' total manufactured exports. Second, it is in countries that had the highest rates of industrial export growth that female employment increased fastest in the 1970s. South Korea and the Philippines, countries that have had particularly high rates of growth of manufactured exports, have had exceptionally fast growth of female relative to male industrial employment, as, to a lesser extent, have Tunisia, Hong Kong, and Colombia. In consequence, countries now exporting a large share of their industrial output (i.e., the Asian NICs and countries like Tunisia) have high shares of female workers in their industrial labor force.

The importance of industrial export growth as an influence on female industrial employment is evident in the case of the largest developing countries as well as in the small, which have always been more open to trade. Growth in female industrial employment in developing countries depends largely on what happens in China and India, just as a matter of arithmetic, for between them they account for almost seventy percent of the developing countries' female industrial labor force. In both of these cases there has been a marked increase in total trade and in the share of industrial goods exported along with the relatively fast growth of female industrial employment. Brazil, which, untypically for Latin America, had strong growth of female employment, also had the same experience. Total exports were only four percent of the gross national product (GNP) in China in 1961 and five percent of the GNP in Brazil in 1960, but by 1982 the shares had reached ten percent and nine percent, respectively. Indian total exports increased less, from five to six percent from 1960 to 1982. Within these totals, the importance of manufactures increased very markedly in all cases, rising from twenty-six to fifty-two percent in China between 1970 to 1980, from three to forty-one percent in Brazil between 1960 and 1981, and from forty-five to fifty-nine percent of total exports in India between 1960 and 1981 (China 1982; World Bank 1984a). In China, the share of light industry in total industrial output increased markedly, from forty-three percent in 1978 to fifty-two percent in 1981 (China 1982), consistent with the rapid growth of Chinese manufactured exports; textiles and garments accounted for forty percent of the total in 1981 (World Bank, 1984a). Indian manufactured exports are concentrated on textiles and garments to a similar degree, while Brazilian exports also consist mainly of light industrial goods, though leaning to electronics rather than textiles and garments. In all of these countries, the familiar pattern of female occupational segregation occurs, with women predominating in light industrial production. Even in China, where women are more widely employed throughout industry than in most other countries, women are nevertheless concentrated in food processing, textiles, and, especially, the clothing and leather industries, where fifty-nine percent of the total labor force in State-owned units was female in 1980, compared with thirty-two percent of the industrial labor force as a whole (China 1982). It is therefore fully predictable that in all three countries, strong growth of exports of manufactures should have led to relatively strong growth of female industrial employment.

The experience of different Latin American countries in respect to female industrial employment is particularly interesting. It covers a whole range of experiences, illuminating the disproportionate employment benefits and costs for women of export expansion on the one hand and of industrial stagnation on the other.

Industrialization in the larger countries, primarily Brazil, was not strongly adversely affected in the 1970s by international conditions for two reasons. While the demand for industrial products was mainly local, policies were introduced to increase international competitiveness and industrial exports, and female employment increased significantly. We have seen that female industrial employment growth was quite strong as a result. But smaller countries were more vulnerable to international conditions, and others (e.g., Venezuela) were still in an intermediate position, trying to overcome a previous dependence on mineral exports as their reserves were depleted. Both of the last two groups were at the strategically difficult point of having a manufacturing sector that was both more dependent on imported inputs of fuel and materials than the Asian economies and less competitive internationally (the Asian economies had begun to promote exports much earlier). From the mid-1970s, their general economic growth and industrial expansion was considerably cut back, and total industrial employment either fell absolutely or grew relatively slowly thereafter in international terms.

In the Latin American and Caribbean countries among the eighteen developing countries for which data are available, the three with the lowest rates of increases of industrial output and industrial employment (Venezuela, Jamaica, and Haiti) actively *substituted* male for female labor in industry. As employment conditions tightened (against a background of previously high unemployment), women were squeezed out of industrial jobs: the absolute number of jobs for women in industry fell, while it rose for men. In Haiti between 1974 and 1983 and Jamaica between 1974 and 1981, the number of women employed in manufacturing fell by the same proportion, seventeen percent, while the number of men employed increased by twenty-two percent in the first case and eighteen percent in the second (ILO 1984). Sri Lanka, despite its location, is comparable in its economic structure to the smaller Latin American economies, with heavy reliance on primary product exports and a newly and only weakly established modern industrial sector; this did not prove sufficiently competitive internationally to thrive in the difficult conditions of the late 1970s. Industrial sector employment declined there absolutely as well from 1974 to 1980 (without any significant compensating expansion of employment in other sectors) and that part of the industrial labor force that suffered disproportionate job loss was the women workers.

The experience of Taiwan, for which data are available separately, finally reinforces the point that in times of economic reversal, women bear the brunt of loss of employment. In 1974 and 1975, Taiwan, like the other NICs, suffered from the first oil price shock and manufacturing employment fell back sharply. Women's employment fell by fourteen percent, compared with eight percent among men. Mainly, this was a consequence of the immediate impact of the sudden slowdown of world trade—the world rate of growth of manufactured exports fell back in 1974–75, never to regain the momentum of the 1960s and early 1970s. The export industries in Taiwan, which are also the most "feminized" (leather goods, toys, electricals and electronics, plastics, and clothing) were the worst hit by the recession. But in most other industries too, where women were not particularly important in the industrial labor force, job loss was felt disproportionately among them.

There was an across-the- board bias against female workers when jobs suddenly became scarcer.

Despite such setbacks, the number of jobs for women in the manufacturing industry in developing countries has been increasing faster since about 1960 than it has for men, and as a result, the share of women in the total manufacturing labor force in developing countries has risen overall. In terms of crude job creation, women have thus relatively benefited in this sector, and it is argued that this has been due in large part to developing economies' increased supply of manufactured goods to international markets.

But crude job creation is an inadequate index for assessing the value for women of changes in manufacturing employment even if we take for granted that wage employment has an absolute value of its own for women as a means to emancipation. For a start, the employment statistics from which the quantitative statements derive are incomplete as a measure of renumerated work. Second, most of the new jobs have been created in a small number of countries, so that women in the majority of developing countries have not benefited relatively from recent industrialization. There is also some evidence that on balance the *quality* of employment on offer to women has been deteriorating relatively to that available to men; that does not necessarily imply an absolute deterioration in the conditions of work available to women over time. Finally, the increase in industrial employment opportunities for women due to increased international integration has rested on an explicit inferiority of treatment of female labor compared to male. How do all these qualifications modify the generally positive picture of female employment in manufacturing that a focus on the numbers of new factory jobs alone suggests?

There is a bias in official employment statistics toward recording large-scale, factory employment. Work in small, less formally organized and little regulated operations and individual employment of an erratic or casual kind are underrepresented. In principle, it is quite possible that the apparent relative increase in total female employment in industry is spurious. If, traditionally, women informally employed in small-scale industrial activities have lost work because their products have been superseded by factory products, the reduction in their number should offset the number of factory jobs created. But if their work had been unrecorded in the statistics, then the subtraction is not done and the supposed scale of job creation is an overestimate. If men are not displaced from the informal sector to the same degree by the expansion of factory industry then women's apparently increased presence in the manufacturing labor force and relatively greater benefit from industrialization could be an illusion.

The displacement of women's work in rural industrial activities, mainly food processing, is quite well established. Much of the disadvantage rural women have suffered through the introduction of modern technology has in fact been in industrial rather than agricultural activities: the case of women rice-huskers of Indonesia, whose livelihood was wiped out by the introduction of rice mills, is perhaps the best known. But displacement of wage work opportunities for women has probably been much less serious in urban industry. Many manufactured goods are new products supplied to new markets. They do not displace products sold locally and by extension do not displace the local producers of such goods. The export sector, which clearly produces for new markets, is where incremental female employment has been concentrated, as we have seen. Electronics products (both consumer goods and components) are the most obvious totally new product category. Though mostly exported, they might be said, by stretching the imagination, to have displaced local traditional musicians and orators (but are just as likely to have stimulated demand for these services). But otherwise they have had no displacement effect. The young women employed in electronics would previously in many countries merely have married earlier; they have not in any meaningful sense deprived others (or themselves) of alternative employment. Much exported clothing is also of goods not made previously or not suitable for the local market, being of higher price and quality or of "fashionable" design or both.

Food processing and plastics are probably the two main female labor force industries that *have* displaced female workers in the informal sector. As in rural areas, much urban food processing is traditionally done by women commercially as well as for domestic consumption; their livelihoods may well have been cut back by increased factory food production. Some factory food production is again for export, however, and furthermore factory production itself introduces a new type of demand for processed foods in the shape of ready-to-eat street foods for factory workers. Preparation of these foods is an expanding informal sector activity in which women predominate in many countries (Cohen 1986). Cheap plastic goods have superseded many traditional utensils such as baskets, pottery, and cutlery, some previously made by women. But the production of metal cutlery, for example, is a male occupation, so the displacement effect has not fallen only on women. The net effect by sex will be difficult to judge and probably varies from country to country.

On balance, taking the main female-employing industries (garments, electronics, food processing, and plastics) together, it therefore seems unlikely that there has been a significant displacement of women informal sector workers. Also, male employment creation, predominantly in heavy industry, is very unlikely to have displaced female informal sector workers to any significant degree. Metal products, automobiles, chemicals, and the like are in the main also product innovations that, when they do substitute for indigenous female-produced materials (e.g., fertilizers for dung, traditionally collected by women in the Middle East, India, and Africa) so enhance total productivity that the work opportunities they create far outweigh loss of value from traditional activities—largely done, of course, by unpaid women. Moreover, the displacement effect frequently falls on men doing traditional work (e.g., when carts are replaced by trucks), so that to argue selectively that women are the only victims of such changes is not convincing. The judgment that total net job creation in industry has favored female employment can stand.

The second reason why the quantitative assessment of female employment changes is not necessarily undermined when the biases of official statistics are taken into account is that changes in informal sector industrial employment do not always reduce women's wage work opportunities. Indeed, statistical bias may lead in some cases to an *underestimate* rather than an overestimate of total net job creation for women. There is some evidence that total employment opportunities for women in manufacturing industry may have been increased by an expansion of outwork. The increase in street food is one example. More importantly, domestic outworkers carrying out piecework operations can in some industries substitute satisfactorily for factory employees, where the production line does not have to be physically integrated, the machinery and equipment used may not be too large to be used in a domestic setting and may not be in need of constant technical monitoring, and quality-control standards do not have to be too exacting. Many processes meet these conditions, especially in light industrial assembly type operations; the clothing industry is a major example but not the only one (IDS 1981). Women make up the bulk of domestic outworkers, basically because domestic piecework is a way of reconciling unpaid household work (especially child care), which, though time consuming is often of an intermittent nature, with wage labor. (In addition, women can also have older children take part in the work, so that outwork is one of the commonest ways in which children can earn some income for household.)

The reasons for supposing that outwork may have been increasing in recent years as a consequence of recession have already been mentioned. Many authors believe that such an expansion has been taking place; Portes and Benton (1984) have surveyed the literature and developed broad estimates. Most of the evidence comes from Latin America, the region where, as we have seen, growth of formal sector industrial employment for women has been weakest—and where in some countries there has been an actual decline. In Latin America, the informal sector is larger and more important as a source of work for women than in any other region (Boserup 1970), so there is probably a high base level of domestic outwork and industrial contracting in any case. But the evidence for increase in these activities as presented by Portes and Benton is quite convincing and is further reinforced when the international market situation is considered. As we have seen, Latin America export suppliers have tended to be marginally competitive internationally; hence, they have probably suffered more than most from fluctuating sales.

It is possible, therefore, that there has not in fact been a fall in the total *numbers* of women employed in Latin American industries but rather a change in the relative proportions of factory and, mostly unrecorded, domestic outworkers, with the latter increasing. At any rate, the formal sector employment figures certainly *underestimate* the number of industrial jobs for women. In terms of numbers of women employed, the regional situation may not have been as bad for women as it seems from official statistics of the 1970s.

Consideration of outwork may redress a little the fact that new industrial jobs for women in developing countries in the past twenty years or so have been heavily concentrated in Asia, particularly East and South Asia. In a sense, concentration of new employment for women in particular regions and countries does not matter *unless* the improvement for women in one region has been had at the expense of those in another. Insofar as the increasing internationalization of industrial production lies behind increases in female employment, it is arguable that Asian gains *have* up to a point necessarily entailed Latin American losses. However, if there has been an increase in informal sector industrial outwork for women in Latin America, the overall world picture would not appear to be dismal.

Counting the *numbers* of people in employment is only half the story, however. The other aspect is the conditions of their work. For a start, domestic outwork has the worst conditions in the industrial sector; it is essentially insecure, with the lowest piece-rate wages and without any of the non-output-related benefits that are to a greater or lesser extent the due of women in factory employment (though of course more routinely attainable by men). It is arguable also that in different ways the feminized industries in the formal sector offer work in worse conditions than the average in manufacturing. The clothing and textiles industry, particularly clothing, operates in relatively small premises often immune to the labor and occupational safety laws that do something to ensure minimal standards in larger factories (ILO 1980). In the electronics industry, considerable occupational hazards are presented by work with many toxic substances and with microscopes; workers are generally protected from the toxic materials, but eye disorders are frequently reported (Lim 1981, Eisold 1984).

There are of course also damaging working conditions in male-based industries, for instance, in steel and coal mining, and it is not easy to claim that women have a monopoly on unpleasant and harmful tasks in manufacturing. No other industry, however, dispenses with the members of its work force as electronics does, after a mere five to ten years, nor presents them with such unstable prospects of employment from year to year. For women who only wish for paid employment for a relatively few years between school and marriage, this limitation on length of employment may not be a problem. But many others want and need to continue to earn wages, and for them being ejected from the electronics labor force is disastrous, because often few wage-earning opportunities exist for women in the local labor market (Lim 1981). Employment insecurity has far more damaging consequences for female workers than it does for male workers in such circumstances.

The terms of women's work in developing country industry may well have also *deteriorated* relatively in recent years with the recession (quite apart from a shift to outwork). The effect is again attributable to tighter conditions in international markets. Data on employment conditions in South Korean industry illustrate what may have been happening more widely for women who remain in factory employment—perhaps even more strongly in other countries without South Korean manufacturing industry's competitive edge. Hours worked increased significantly in all three major export industries in the recessionary years 1976 and 1980, whereas they had been falling previously in each case. The intensity of work in manufacturing was increased and wages per hour, while increasing in nominal terms, did not rise as much proportionally as at other periods. Evidence from a number of developing countries combined is not inconsistent with this as a general possibility (UNIDO 1983). In the few industrial branches for which information was available, the wage gap between developed and developing countries increased between 1970 and 1978 (a period spanning the first recession). The wage gap widened most in the feminized, light industrial (food and textiles) branches; longitudinal data on relative hours worked are not available, unfortunately, but in 1978 textile workers worked the longest hours.

One potential source of employment insecurity for women seems *not* to have been very important, despite common allegations to the contrary: A recent study of female employment in TNCs comes to the conclusion that TNCs have not been markedly "footloose," that is they have not in practice closed down operations in particular countries and laid off work forces permanently in response to rising local wages or to heightened wage claims (ILO/UNCTC 1985). Production facilities tend to be upgraded in conformity with changing factor cost ratios rather than closed down altogether. Thus, a plant for manufacturing simple radios would be retooled to produce higher valued videocassette recorders, for example, and a new facility for making radios would be set up elsewhere in a lower wage location. Women's employment opportunities are modified over time therefore in any one location, while not in general curtailed completely.

Outright job loss represents in a sense the ultimate deterioration in conditions of employment. There is a proposition, dating from Karl Marx, that women, as the "reserve" part of the labor force, are drawn into formal employment only when male labor is no longer available and are the first to be expelled from the labor force when job opportunities fall back. The cross-country data show that women *are* drawn into the manufacturing labor force most rapidly when growth of total employment is fastest and the availability of male labor most stretched. Thus, the positive part of Marx's prediction is fulfilled to that extent. There is less evidence on the negative side of what happens when total employment falls back. Studies of the industrialized countries show that women lost employment disproportionately in manufacturing in the mid-1970s but that in aggregate this was more than compensated for by continued expansion of the service sector and female jobs there (OECD 1976). Women lost on the swings but gained on the roundabouts of occupational segregation.

In the developing countries in the 1970s, including the recessionary years, female industrial employment growth was relatively slow (even sometimes negative) where total employment grew slowly. The one case (Taiwan) where detailed data on branch level employment changes by sex are available also shows that in the situation of sharp, sudden cutback, female employment declines were larger than male in aggregate and in most branches (see p. 96). The service sector in developing countries, though also offering many jobs for women, is much smaller than in the industrialized countries and cannot have provided compensating new jobs to the same extent as in the OECD countries. One reason why female industrial employment may be relatively vulnerable is that in all branches, even the less feminized ones, women are concentrated in direct production jobs (archetypically in production assembly lines as opposed to design, supervisory, and maintenance positions). Demand for direct production labor fluctuates more closely with the actual level of firm's operations than demand for other types of labor. Other principles may apply within firms and industries in determining layoffs, for example, the "last in, first out" rule. Such rules are not necessarily sexually discriminatory in intent, even if the outcome is uneven as between male and female workers. However, the evidence on sex differences in labor turnover rates is contradictory, which suggests that application of the last in, first out rule should not in practice lead to a systematic bias against female labor. Layoffs may well be imposed in a purely discriminatory way, trading on the fact that women are considered more "docile" than male workers, and docility extends to a relative lack of protest at layoffs (Elson and Pearson 1980).

There is plenty of evidence—in developed countries at any rate—of the widespread acceptance of the view that women should have less access to employment when jobs are scarce. This view springs directly from the "male breadwinner" ethic: family welfare is held to be less damaged when a woman loses her job than when a man does, on the presumption that his wage is larger. In family *income* terms, when there is a sex wage differential, this is true. But in terms of the interests of industrial employers, the opposite applies; given equivalent productivity, employers should tend to dismiss *male* workers. If the competitive pressures that in general lead employers to prefer cheaper female labor in certain industries are overturned in times of recessionary contraction, that would testify to the greater power of cultural forces than economic ones in times of crisis, mediated of course by the established position of male labor.

In conclusion, recent industrialization in developing countries has incorporated women into the sectoral work force to an unprecedented extent. But it is at least arguable (though all of these propositions need wider empirical verification) that women's conditions of employment in industry are inferior to men's in various dimensions; that they have been worsening in periods of recession; and that when there has been retraction in industry, women have suffered disproportionate loss of work. More certainly, it is undoubtedly the case that women are concentrated in low-grade, relatively unskilled jobs without significant promotion prospects and that women's access to employment is severely limited in many industrial branches. Women also have lower earnings than men in industry to a greater extent than can be explained by this pattern of differentiation. In sum, women have an inferior position in employment in the industrial sector even in the one new high-technology branch, electronics, where they are employed in large numbers. That the increased incorporation of women into the industrial labor force will not in itself guarantee any improvement in their position in that sector is suggested by two further observations. Occupational segregation by sex in Britain has not diminished over seventy years (Hakim 1979). Women's lesser technical and scientific qualifications are likely to prevent them from entering the newest, high-productivity, high-wage expanding branches. The fast growing Asian countries are increasing their capacity in "science-based" industries, which will have increasing weight in the industrial sector in terms of both the number of jobs and the wages they offer. If women do not enter these new industries, women's earnings in the industrial sector will probably begin to fall on average relative to men's.

The increase in women's participation in developing country industry over the past twenty years has therefore reinforced—certainly not undermined—sexual stratification in the labor market. Even if the level of articipation continues to increase, the quality of women's employment can only decline further relative to men's unless women enter high-wage-paying jobs in the highly productive manufacturing activities for which access to technical education and training is a prerequisite. Occupational segregation has to be broken down not only to allow women access to these jobs but to give the incentive for technical training. Women will otherwise continue to be confined to labor-intensive, low-wage-paying work while men's wages rise on average. Furthermore, the presently feminized jobs will become less important in the industrial structure as economies evolve beyond the stage of labor-intensive manufacture. And women will be in a weak position to hold on to employment even in the presently feminized industries if radical technological changes should be introduced and mechanize the production of, for example, garments. It is crucial for women's social position that they challenge their subordination in industrial labor markets before an era of labor surplus reemerges with the generalized use of labor-saving technology.

7

Services

The services sector is heterogeneous in the types of economic activities it covers and in its relation to the international economy. It includes large modern sector enterprises, such as tourism, and small black market enterprises, many so hidden that they escape any form of statistical record; one-to-one personal health and educational services as well as services to organizations; directly traded activities and others for purely local consumption; national scale traders, including wholesalers as well as neighborhood suppliers, such as small local shopkeepers and itinerant street hawkers; and all forms of transport and communications. It is impossible to find systematic economic causes of the overall growth of such a mixed bag of activities. But, nevertheless, the individual activities can be sorted into those that bear a direct or indirect relationship to international markets and those that have only the most tenuous connection, and some generalizations about the impact of changes in the international environment can be made on that basis.

It is unfortunate, if not surprising in view of the heterogeneity of the services sector, that very little study has been made of the causes of growth and employment and the nature of work and the sexual division of labor in services. It is in many countries not only the largest employment sector in total but particularly important in providing jobs for women. In developed countries, fifty-seven percent of all employed women worked in the service sector in 1980; they accounted for forty-nine percent of the sectoral work force, a higher proportion than their representation in the labor force as a whole (forty percent) (ILO/INSTRAW 1985) and a higher share than in any other sector. In developing countries taken altogether (where agricultural employment is still overwhelmingly predominant as the source of employment for men and women alike), seventeen percent of all employed women worked in services, where they represented twenty-seven percent of the sectoral labor force (in this case, in aggregate, being slightly underrepresented in this sector) (ILO/INSTRAW 1985). But the problem of statistical underestimation is probably more severe in this sector than elsewhere. Many of the personal services in particular are small scale and informal, and a disproportionate amount of such work is done by women. As a result, this is one case where not too much credence should be put on the quantitative estimates.

Official statistics, even so, reveal that female participation in this sector is very high in some parts of the developing world. Latin America and the Caribbean are considerably out of line with the rest. Although the rate of female labor force participation is the lowest of all regions here, and women accounted for only twenty-three percent of the total labor force in 1980, women are thirty-nine percent of the labor in services, and the sector provided employment for fully seventy percent of the entire female labor force. In both Africa and Asia, the services sector is not only a smaller part of the national economy in terms of output and employment but it also employs fewer women; services occupied twenty percent and nineteen percent of the total labor force in Africa and Asia, respectively, in 1980, and women were only twenty-seven and twenty-four percent, respectively, of the sectoral labor force, *below* their representation in the total labor force in each case.

There are three parts of the service sector where women tend to be particularly heavily represented: the community services (health, education, and social welfare), commerce (retail services), and domestic service. Their presence in community services as nurses, teachers, and social workers is often explained as an extension of women's "nurturing" role into the public domain. Nevertheless, considerable numbers of men take work in this area in the developing countries. Women's employment in domestic service is even more obviously open to the same interpretation, but here again, in developing countries, in Asia particularly, women do not have the monopoly on such paid employment. Women's presence in retail trade is in fact in some places more truly an extension of their other work. In Africa, notably, women are largely responsible for food production, and this spills over into women's predominance in the distribution of foodstuffs, in both rural and urban areas, as they market produce superfluous to their own household's needs. In Latin America, women also predominate in retail trade in the exceptionally large domestic service category, but the reasons for this are related to their opportunities in other sectors in a different way. The service sector is virtually the only place where most women can expect to find any kind of paid work in Latin America, since they have effectively been excluded from agriculture and (though this is changing in Brazil and other industrial exporting countries) from modern industry. So women migrating from the rural areas where there is little paid employment for them end up offering their labor in the service sector. This occupational crowding tends to push them into the informal, ill-paid end of the range of jobs available in the sector, of which domestic service, "entertainment," and retail jobs are the main examples.

Women are also employed in public administration and clerical work within the services sector, but the number of opportunities open to them here varies considerably from country to country. Their importance is greatest in these areas in the developed countries, where secretarial work, for example, is almost a completely feminized occupation (though this is beginning to break down as higher general unemployment drives some men to pioneer a breakthrough into an occupation that is quite well paid in relation to average total earnings). Women are a much lower proportion of office workers in the developing countries in general. This regional distinction applies to other public sector occupations too, where women tend similarly to be more important in developed than in developing countries. Among teachers, for instance, women were approximately sixty-five percent of primary school teachers in developed countries in 1980 as against forty-five percent in developing countries; they were thirty-eight as against thirty percent of secondary school teachers, and twenty-eight as against twenty-three percent of third level teachers.

The prestigiousness (and pay) of teachers rises with the level of the educational establishment, so that these data also show that women in both developed and developing countries are concentrated at the lower end of the job scale in the educational sector. The same applies in other branches of public community services and in the private sector—

thus, throughout the services sector as a whole. Women are far more important as nurses and paramedics than doctors; they are found in the lower echelons of the public administration; they are clerical workers rather than managers, telephonists rather than telephone engineers, etc. They are the mainstay of the worst paid jobs in the services sector, broadly defined (domestic service and the retail trade), and are furthermore most probably disproportionately concentrated in the underestimated gray informal sector end of the spectrum into which such employ spills over. No data are available on wages, but it seems very likely that the earnings differential by sex is in fact higher in the services sector than in any other.

These various services vary in their openness to international markets. Some services are directly traded—for consistency, we should in fact properly treat these as comprising a market all of their own, alongside the markets in goods, finance, and technology, but the paucity of information makes this unrealistic. Shipping, passenger and freight air transport, tourism, financial brokerage services, insurance, and telecommunications are examples of activities that are carried out internationally in their own right. Trade in these services has expanded like that in other international markets, and national involvement has been shown to be most buoyant where there is a comparative advantage, just as in trade in goods. Human capital, that is, a skilled and competent labor force, is the primary ingredient for success in services (Sapir and Lutz 1981). Developed countries are most strongly represented in the field of services of this kind, and the United States in particular is pressing, in accordance with its own potential dominance of the markets, for greater liberalization in international trade in services, which is presently more protected than the market in goods has become. At present, only a very few developing countries have any sizable presence in the international services market with the exception of tourism.

A larger number of developing countries have quite a range of important service activities that indirectly supply international markets. These consist of services supplied to facilitate the movement of goods destined for international markets: even though the services are provided for the internal movement of goods within national boundaries (and thus are not themselves traded internationally) they are linked to the quantity of visible trade. The same share of output of the commercial, transport, and communications parts of the service sector might be directly attributable to international markets as international trade represented twenty-three percent of total output of middle-income countries in 1982 (World Bank 1984a). (Imported as well as exported goods require handling in this way, of course, but usually the ratio of exports to output is comparable with the ratio of imports in consumption, so it is sufficient to take account only of the export ratio.) It is in this sense that it has been estimated that export expansion accounted for twenty-seven percent of the expansion of employment in the services sector as a whole in the Taiwanese economy between 1971 and 1976 (Kuo n.d.). Taiwan is one of the most important exporters among developing countries—indeed of all countries—with fifty percent of total output exported, so that international markets are unlikely to have been as important a cause of expansion of the services sector in many other places, but nevertheless the estimate suggests that the contribution will have been at least significant elsewhere.

Last, there are a set of services that are not integrally connected with international markets and that are influenced by them only indirectly in various ways via the pressures exerted by international factors on the general configuration of the economy. The domestically oriented trade-facilitating services (commerce, transport, and communications without any international connections) are affected only in so far as the international economy contributes to the growth of total effective demand in an economy—which of course it does, most importantly, though the precise effect is difficult to quantify. Public sector expenditure on social, health, and educational services, and, therefore, the level and terms of employment in these services, may come under pressure if public expenditure has to be restrained. Conditions incurred by the burden of heavy external indebtedness, for example, lead developing countries' economic policy to be modified in this way.

There is also a range of personal services the demand and supply of which reflect the influence of international factors (if any) not on government policy but on the level and distribution of personal income in a society. In national economies where the average level of national income per capita is relatively high, but the dispersion of income is quite wide, persons and households at the upper end of the scale command incomes that are a multiple of the subsistence level of income prevalent at the bottom. Any upward movement in the average income or any widening in its dispersion (by either an increase in higher incomes or decline in the lower, or both) increases the effective "human services" purchasing power of upper income groups. The adjustment process many debtor countries are having to undertake increases income inequality because of declines in real wages, employment, and investment.

Technological changes affect communications, of course, and also administrative and secretarial work, through the vastly superior capability of handling and processing information brought by microelectronics. A number of studies have been done of impact of microelectronics on the latter area (for reference see Schmitz 1985), which despite some initial "catastrophizing" about the social effects and the effect on labor use in particular, has come in the end to a fairly balanced conclusion. While some tasks and even occupations are indeed entirely eliminated, increased capability has generated so much extra activity in new as well as old service functions that the aggregate net effect has been to increase the demand for labor. (The analogy with the impact of modern high-yielding varieties in agriculture is striking.) The effect on women specifically is not clear, but there is at least no evidence in the developed countries, to which the introduction of the new techniques has largely been confined, of any major displacement.

The impact of technological changes has been limited to those activities within the service sector (setting aside the introduction of household appliances, which has allowed female participation to rise in industry and in community services without generating a fully equivalent rise in demand for paid domestic service). Elsewhere in the sector, the impact on female employment has rested on the direct or indirect effect of international goods and financial markets.

Developing countries that have grown by rapid expansion of exports of manufacture will have generated complementary employment in trade-related service activities, such as transport and communications. But the majority of the main exporting countries are in Asia, where the service sector is not in total particularly large and where women are less than proportionally represented in the sectoral labor force compared with their participation in the labor force as a whole. It is also the case that generally this part of the services sector is not an important source of jobs for women, so if it has expanded relative to other service activities probably it will not have been to the particular benefit of female employment. Nevertheless, some employment for women will probably have been created in the clerical and secretarial occupations within this part of the service sector.

The growth of international financial transactions also seems unlikely to have generated much work for women in this sector, except again in secretarial positions in banks and brokerages in developed countries. Women are not well represented in higher level jobs in these enterprises. Nor is the financial sector per se of much importance outside the developed countries, with the exception perhaps of Hong Kong, Singapore, and tax havens.

Tourism is one area where female employment is fairly extensive, in catering, hotel, and entertainment work. Prostitution to foreign males is also a major business in some countries, Thailand being perhaps the best known. In all of these kinds of activity there has been an underlying trend of considerable expansion of business in aggregate worldwide but with great fluctuations from year to year and between countries. Gains for total and female employment in any one place therefore tend to be highly insecure, as well as very seasonal, and in the case of prostitution, and many entertainments, of a peculiarly degrading kind.

In many developed countries that are trying to stem the secular rise in public expenditure as a proportion of national income, and in the large number of developing countries that are heavily externally indebted, there have been attempts in recent years to cut back public services and employment. Women are important in the labor force in these activities, more so in developed than developing countries.

There is an incomplete analogy with female employment in industry here, in terms of the incentives on the employer to differentiate between male and female employees when it comes to retrenchment. On the one hand, women in the low-ranking services jobs are roughly equivalent to the female direct-production workers in manufacturing. (In this case, being in the front line consists of directly servicing personal clients, rather than being in managerial and administrative positions.) This factor would make women more liable to dismissal when the level of services (output) is absolutely cut back and more vulnerable to deterioration in working conditions when the *quality* of services is reduced and more services have to be delivered by a given number of workers. The counteracting incentive is, moreover, probably less strong than in industry: the wage differential by sex is likely to be less marked in the public than the private sector. Governments, as employers, would be expected to conform more rigorously than other employers to the equal wage legislation to which increasing numbers of them nominally subscribe (93 out of 139 countries in the world as of 1983) (Sivard 1985). It should be mentioned, however, that there is apparently *more* wage discrimination by sex in the public than in the private sector in one African country anyway (Knight and Sabot 1982). On balance, therefore, women would seem to be more vulnerable in principle to job loss in the services sector than in industry, since they would not even have cheapness to recommend them. But in industry, the outcome is *against* women, so the result may not be any worse relatively speaking in the public community services. What the employment outcome actually has been in countries reducing their public expenditure is certainly a subject deserving investigation.

In Latin America, the services sector is overwhelmingly the largest source of jobs for women, who are concentrated within the sector in domestic service as maids, housekeepers, child minders, etc. The level of employment in this sector has been affected indirectly by international events that have set the parameter constraints on the course of development with increasing severity in recent years. The main influence has been on the labor supply side.

Both agriculture and industry in Latin America have reached a critical point in recent years. Lack of access to markets in the developed countries has held back exports from the region, and production for international markets has not, therefore, expanded in any significant way (with one or two exceptions such as Brazil and, for a time, Colombia); the rate of growth of industrial output was sharply reduced from the early 1970s onwards. Total personal income in these sectors was held back in consequence.

The only route to balance of payments adjustment thus lay in cutting back imports of investment, intermediate, and consumer goods, especially the last. Set against declines in personal income, this meant that the real purchasing power of large segments of the urban and rural population fell. Income distribution is inequitable in Latin America compared with other continents at the best of times (World Bank 1985), with very large proportions of the population living at or below the poverty line. Reductions in real income have desperate consequences for households struggling to survive. One survival strategy is for more members of the household to seek to sell their labor; the low participation rate of Latin American women has meant that they were the main group from whom the increase in labor supply could come. Given that the great majority of women already working were employed in the service sector, largely in domestic service, and that there is a large unregulated "informal" part of the sector where entry is quite unrestricted, most women newly seeking employment will have looked for work in the service sector.

In the informal sector (in services or in industrial homework, already discussed in Chapter 6), wages are highly sensitive to market conditions (i.e., to the balance of labor supply and demand). The widespread depression of personal income in Latin American countries in the early 1980s probably contributed to a decline in the demand for labor in the informal personal services sector, so that with an influx of female labor combined with a likely decline in demand, the prevailing wage level has probably fallen in real terms. An important secondary effect will probably be at least partly beneficial for female employment, however. Since individual formal sector incomes are not so subject to variation in response to market conditions, a consequence of the increased supply of labor to the informal sector will likely be an *increase* in the ratio of formal sector to informal sector wages (an intensification of personal income inequality). The purchasing power of higher formal sector earners would also probably rise in terms of the cost of personal services, by the same token. This income effect, while shockingly indicative of the disparity in individual incomes, should at least be conducive to some increase in the demand for the sorts of services provided by female labor. The ill effect of international economic pressure on the poorest may be slightly alleviated in this way. But again this is a subject that deserves urgent investigation in view of the importance of service sector employment to women in Latin America and the fact that the survival of low-income families is greatly dependent on the earnings generated by women. (Reduction in inequality in Colombian cities during the more buoyant 1970s was attributable mainly to increased female participation [Urrutia 1984].) Moreover, the number of female-headed households, and thus of children dependent on their mother's income, is very high in this region.

Part IV

THE NEED FOR A
REASSESSMENT

8

Emerging Trends in the International Economy as Related to Women: Summary of Findings

The purpose of this study has been to assess the extent to which the emergence of a modern international economy has contributed to development needs relating to the economic position of women. Only by identifying the trends at work and their effects is it possible to suggest the appropriate directions for policy. Beneficial market tendencies should be reinforced; measures to *realize* their potential benefit should be introduced; harmful policy measures or market tendencies should be modified by introducing effective countervailing measures, and tendencies that are to the advantage of one set of countries but that have specifically deleterious social consequences, in this case for women, should be compensated.

Taking the long view, one of the most remarkable features of the postwar period has been the expansion of international markets relative to national markets and the expanding influence of the international market forces. In the longer term, there has been increased integration and interdependence among national economies, large and small, developed and developing, tantamount to the emergence of a modern world economy. Concomitantly, women's economic participation, particularly in developing countries, has been affected in all sectors by this heightened exposure to the international economy.

Some indications of the sheer scale of international market expansion are that developing countries' exports of goods have increased

117

more than 3.5 times by value in real terms since 1960, significantly more than their increase in total real income, and gross inflows of medium and long-term capital to these countries have multiplied almost eight times in the shorter period since 1970. The growth of product and financial markets—the latter in particular, which represents a largely new element in the international economy and now dwarfs the scale of trade flow—has presented countries with new opportunities to be exploited and new dangers to be faced. As a result, national economic development is now constrained by international considerations as never before.

Greater international interdependence has undoubtedly contributed to world economic growth over the postwar period. But interdependence also implies vulnerability, and events since 1970 or so have shown not only the inherent fragility of certain aspects of the modern world economy but also the consequences of unequal international economic relations. The resilience of some national economies and indeed of the international economic system itself has been sorely tested, and many developing countries continue to be in precarious positions because of the nature of their involvement with the international economy. The Bretton Woods institutions contributed to the reduction of formal barriers to international trade, and through a series of multilateral negotiations under the auspices of GATT, tariffs on many products have been virtually eliminated. But some markets of special interest to the developing countries, notably textiles and agricultural products, remain heavily protected. Also, complementary efforts by the United Nations Conference on Trade and Development (UNCTAD) to benefit the developing countries have led to the introduction of the generalized system of preferences (GSP), but this has had only a limited effect.

Within the total of postwar world trade, the proportion of manufactures has risen fastest of all. Exports of manufactures have grown even faster from developing than from developed countries (of course from an infinitely smaller base). Some developing countries, known as the newly industrializing countries (NICS) or fast-growing exporters of manufactures, most of them in Asia, now export on average almost sixty percent of their total industrial output, compared with a mere twelve percent twenty years ago. In these countries, which together account for three quarters of the total developing countries' manufactured exports, the expansion of export-oriented manufacturing has led to large increases in female employment in industry, frequently in economic free trade zones.

The expansion of the international financial market is perhaps the most remarkable phenomenon of postwar economic developments. From being roughly on a par with goods transactions, financial flows are now about twenty times as large. Their role has gone far beyond merely underpinning physical trade to supplying capital and credit for investment and for speculation across the exchanges. The existence of this new market has, however, proved something of a hornet's nest for many developing countries. By borrowing in the mid-1970s, these countries continued to support balance of payments deficits to maintain levels of consumption and production commensurate with the productive base built up in previous years. The consequence was that in an international economic environment that became increasingly hostile and nonexpansionary, the debt piled up and quickly preempted an extremely high portion of foreign exchange earnings for its repayment. Developing countries' total external debt increased five times between 1974 and 1984; by 1983 it represented about twenty-five percent of developing countries' total national income, debt service took about twenty-two percent of major borrowers' export earnings, and the trend was rising steeply. The net direction of financial flow took a historic turn in 1982 when outpayments from the largest, most heavily indebted developing countries exceeded inflows of new money for the first time as debt repayments took their toll.

Greater international economic activity has contributed substantially to world economic growth and to the improvement of material standards in many countries over the past four decades. International expansion is thus partly responsible for the increases in average life expectancy and levels of education enjoyed by women as well as men in developing countries over this period. But interdependence always carries with it an implicit vulnerability. In the most recent period, there has been a serious deterioration in the international economic environment for developing countries (apart from the special case of the capital surplus oil-exporting countries, which account for a tiny proportion of the world's population). Events since 1970 or so have shown up the inherent fragility of the modern world economy and the damaging consequences to the developing countries of unequal international economic relations. Many developing countries continue to be in a critically difficult position.

In accordance with the predominance of industrialized countries in the world economy, the instability in international markets and the two world recessions since 1970 have been due largely to the measures taken by them to address—scarcely yet to correct—their own internal economic imbalances. The fundamental problem was the decline in the rate of increase of productivity in some of these countries. Industrialized countries have attempted to bring down inflation and raise their growth rate with highly damaging international ramifications. One landmark in the international setting, initiating the explosive growth of financial markets, was a direct consequence of the declining relative strength of the lead position of the United States economy, following the abandonment of gold convertability of the dollar and of fixed exchange rates in 1971. Another disturbing factor was the diversion of resources with the stepping up of the arms race and the Vietnam War, which added to inflationary pressures and started a round of extreme fluctuations in commodity prices. Since the early 1970s, the prices of many non-oil primary commodities have first boomed then collapsed to historic lows. By contrast, the prices of manufactures rose steadily on the world market throughout the period. At the end of the 1970s, the industrialized countries' primary objective became the reduction of inflation, and the consequent shift in monetary policy, together with the need to attract funds to finance public deficits, brought in a new era in the international capital market. The world price of money (the rate of interest), having been very low in real terms throughout the 1970s, rose markedly in 1980 and 1981 and has remained at historically high levels ever since. The one major price movement in this period not determined by the industrialized countries was the multiple increase in the price of oil in 1973 and 1978–79, brought about by the developing oil-exporting countries. The oil price rises undoubtedly aggravated the industrial countries' economic difficulties—though they conferred some short-term benefits too, in the shape of increased oil company profits and higher tax revenues—but they were not the fundamental cause of their problems nor of the world recession.

The quantity of goods traded has been somewhat more stable, generally matching the pattern of world growth of output and income: that is, after an abrupt decline in 1974–75, trade flows recovered, but to slower rates of growth than previously through the rest of the 1970s. Trade volumes, however, sagged seriously from 1981 to 1983. In capital markets, both disbursements and debt continue to increase, but the net *direction* of financial flows took a historic turn in 1982 when outpayments from the largest developing countries most heavily involved in the capital markets exceeded inflows of new money for the first time. These price and volume changes in international markets are attributable in large part to the measures taken by the industrialized countries to cope with their own internal economic problems, which predated, though they were undoubtedly aggravated by, the increase in oil prices in 1973 and 1978–79 and in the 1980s. The effects have been various, depending on the economic structure of the particular developing countries, but in general (apart from the special case of the capital sur- plus OPEC countries, which account for a tiny proportion of the world's population), they have polarized the economic prospects of the three main geographical regions of the developing world: Asia, Africa, and Latin America. Asian countries in general have suffered least: their rates of growth have been reduced with the recessions but have remained positive. In Latin America and Africa, the situation is much worse. Many countries have had actual declines in national income over several years. Fast rates of population increase in both regions have made declines in personal incomes even more severe.

The developing countries in Asia, in particular in East Asia, have the highest ratios of traded goods to national output of all developing countries. The critical feature of their trade pattern in the present con- text is the high share of manufactures in regional exports. Asian coun- tries have thus been operating in the one segment of the international goods market that has seen reasonably sustained growth and stable prices; moreover, they have managed to increase their total share of this market, despite its reduced rate of expansion compared with the 1960s and despite the efforts of other countries to enter it. These Asian countries mostly had not contracted debts on a major scale to get over the first oil shock and the recession of 1974–75, so even after increasing their external borrowing after 1979, their levels of indebtedness were still moderate by international standards. Their economic growth rates have been slower in the 1980s than before, but they are still positive and still higher than those of any other set of developing countries or those of the industrialized countries.

Latin American countries had early on achieved high incomes rela- tive to other developing countries. They mostly built up industrial ca- pacity in the 1960s, producing relatively inefficiently for the home market behind protective barriers. They remained dependent on a range of agricultural and mineral primary commodity exports for for- eign exchange with which to finance their considerable needs for im- ports of oil, industrial inputs, and consumer goods. In the mid-1970s, they were badly affected by the oil price rise combined with the tighter conditions in the world market for developing countries' manufactured exports, which made it difficult for them to diversify their exports in this direction. High commodity prices, however, gave them a basis for borrowing externally to tide them over a transitory period, as seemed likely then, of trade deficits. The rise in interest rates multiplied their level of indebtedness, the collapse in commodity prices cut away the preexisting export revenue base, and the further reductions in world trade in manufactures made even more infeasible the penetration of that market. The cuts in consumption and investment consequent on diversion of resources to service preexisting and new international loans have led to sustained declines in national output and personal income.

The less developed African countries have minimal industrial capacity, and in many cases their productive base is very limited overall. Standards of living above subsistence are dependent on the prices fetched in international markets by exports of traditional primary commodities. With the fall in commodity prices in the 1980s, real incomes have fallen substantially in the continent. Governments have had to resort to external finance to support even minimal levels of consumption. In many cases, their levels of debt are now higher in relation to national income and to export earnings than the Latin American average. Yet the region's capacity to repay remains almost entirely contingent on fluctuating prices and uncertain demand in international commodity markets along with the failing flow of international finances of industrialized countries. Africa's problems have been compounded by crop failures and severe famine, but the underlying international economic constraints remain intractable.

Change in the absolute material position of women naturally reflects the general economic situation in each region. Asian, particularly East Asian, women have shared in the prosperity of their countries, both indirectly as members of households and directly by virtue of the increased amount of paid work available to them. In Latin America and Africa, men and women alike have suffered declines in their standard of living, with the impact being most severe among the poorest people. But, in addition, in Latin American manufacturing and in African agriculture, women's employment prospects have specifically deteriorated during recessions, and there have been inadequate compensating increases in employment opportunities in other sectors. Women have disproportionately borne the brunt of the economic crisis. The loss of better paid income-earning opportunities for women is particularly unfortunate because of the much higher incidence in these two regions than in Asia of women-headed households and the greater dependence of children on women's earnings.

Technology

Product trade and financial transactions have not been the only international variables influencing the level and character of activity in national economies. Technological changes have also been transmitted internationally with profoundly important effects. The scale of these transactions has expanded. The emphasis in studies of technology is usually on the acquisition of modern industrial technology by nation States. But in the recent period, new technology markets have emerged that cut across different sectors, giving developing countries the potential of greater choice in the type of technology to be introduced and, hence, more influence on the future character of their economies. There is, for example, a completely new international arena for exchanges of technology relating to agriculture, and in both agriculture and manufacturing many new product and process technologies have emerged and been widely applied internationally. Some of these technologies may come to be seen historically as being as significant as those of any previous wave of innovations. Microbiological advances, for example, have magnified many times the global capacity for food production; also, the microelectronics revolution is thought by some analysts to be the most likely avenue for lessening the slowdown in the rate of national productivity increase in the developed countries that lay behind the international instability and recessions of the 1970s and 1980s.

As far as women are concerned, the impact of technological change interacting with trade-related factors has varied among economic sectors in its implications for employment. On balance, technological progress in agriculture has not benefited women in developing countries. Most process innovations have led to mechanization of the kinds of tasks usually carried out by women and have in most places reduced employment opportunities for them, especially women from landless families. On the other hand, product innovations, notably the new high-yielding plant varieties, have had a general employment-creating effect from which both men and women have benefited, women arguably more so. The final balance between the two effects is indeterminate, the outcome varying from place to place. It seems that in Asia, where the new varieties of crops have been most widely adopted, the latter tendency has predominated and there has been a net employment-creating effect; however, this effect has been insufficient to absorb all new entrants to the agricultural labor force and stem unemployment. Also, there are disturbing indications that, in South

Asia at least, these increases in production are now provoking faster changes in production *methods,* displacing female labor, so that even here the longer term assessment may show women to have been disadvantaged by technological changes in agriculture.

In industry, the tendencies have been rather different. Technological change in production methods in developing countries has in many cases intensified labor specialization, through the improvement of tools operated manually under labor-intensive methods. This has led not to mechanization or automation leading to massive labor displacement, which has been the predominant type of change in the more advanced industrial structures of the developed countries, but to the creation of new jobs often given to women. Women have accordingly become increasingly important in the industrial labor force of developing countries. In developed countries, the industrial labor force is declining in relative and in absolute size in many places, and there has been a slight decline in the share of women in the total.

In the services sector, new technologies have a complex effect, similar to that in agriculture. The application of microelectronics has revolutionized communication and information processing and handling. Many routine tasks have been superseded as a result, displacing female labor disproportionately. But, at the same time, the general increase in economic activity brought about by the productivity-enhancing effects of technological changes has created new sources of labor demand in many parts of the service sector, for example, the office and commercial sector and the hotel and tourist trade, which are two services clearly influenced by international trading conditions. There may well have ultimately been an increased relative demand for female labor in some developing countries' service sectors. But the impact of technological changes has probably been more limited in the service sector in developing than in developed countries, and employment demand continues to be more importantly shaped by strictly domestic factors having to do with the distribution of personal income, the share of public expenditures in national income, and so on.

Sectoral Changes: Agriculture

The three regions of the developing world differ in their relative abundance of land to population. Africa is—or has been until recently—abundant in land and sparse in population; Asia is short of land relative to the population it carries; and Latin America has a hybrid, dualistic endowment, divided by accident of history and politics into areas carrying a heavy population load on the one hand and extensive, large holdings with few inhabitants on the other.

These varying patterns have differing consequences for women's role in agriculture. Sub-Saharan Africa has been characterized as predominantly having women in its system of cultivation: because human labor is in short supply and cultivable land is not, agriculture, especially of crops for domestic consumption, draws in the whole population to cultivate the land, and women are fully involved. Women rarely take charge of the process, however, even where the men are absent. In large parts of Asia, by contrast, the scarcity of land and surfeit of human labor leads women's marginality to come into play in respect to both title and access to work on the land. In many cases, women work on land in a myriad of tasks for little or no economic reward. As in Africa, women have the responsibility for household-based subsistence production, mostly in small-scale agrobusinesses and poultry and small livestock keeping.

The Latin American pattern is, for the majority of the population, close to the Asian system of agriculture, but men are responsible for more tasks in field cultivation and women have lesser responsibility for food production. The sex selectivity of employment in cash crop and plantation agriculture is, however, close to the African pattern in that it largely, though not entirely, employs men. (In Asia much plantation labor, for example, in tea and rubber, has always been predominantly female.) As a consequence, women's recorded participation rates in agriculture continue to be considered low and unimportant.

Patterns of rural to urban migration are sex selective in different ways in the different continents, as an extension of the use of labor by sex in agriculture. African men's involvement in cash-earning activities inside and outside of agriculture leads many of them to migrate to the towns in search of (often illusory) employment opportunities, while women stay on the land; in South and Southeast Asia, women's wage employment opportunities in plantation agriculture offset their lesser access to agricultural work so that internal migration is more neutral as to sex; and in Latin America, the bulk of employment opportunities are not open to women, and so women migrate to the towns in search of work in larger numbers than men.

Developments in the international economy have intensified the differential characteristics and consequences of these agricultural systems. In Asian agriculture, technological change to increase yields has led to further intensification of cultivation. Improvements in input (seeds, fertilizers, and pesticides) increase the demand for labor, though less than proportionally to the increase in yields. But agricultural mechanization is inherently labor displacing, and it has a tendency moreover to be directed toward the more female-intensive agricultural tasks. By contrast, few technological changes suitable to African conditions have materialized so far, so that, although work patterns have not been modified and women have not been displaced for this reason, agricultural production has fallen far behind population growth and African agricultural productivity has declined relatively. Women's minimal participation in Latin American agriculture has been little affected by technological change in the recent past.

Price movements in international markets have disadvantaged women in agriculture more consistently than technological changes. Agricultural productivity has greatly increased over the past forty years in North America and Europe as well as in parts of Asia; the increase in supplies from these two regions (where population growth is mostly low) has been put onto the world market and has led to a secular decline in the real price of grains on the international market. Most developing countries have, for internal reasons, preferred to keep local food prices down as well. While cheap food has undoubtedly been greatly beneficial to consumers (rural as well as urban), low food prices *can* be detrimental to producers in certain circumstances. The end result for women has consequently varied from region to region.

Where productivity-enhancing technological change has been possible, as in Asia, food producers have suffered less because the increased yields offset lower product prices, and incomes have therefore been maintained. But the employment problem is not solved. First, with the new varieties total labor demand has not risen in the same proportion as output. Second, productivity increases have been less rapid than population growth in many places, and there have been increasing poverty and landlessness among the rural population as a result. Thus, although the female labor participation rate has increased and their share of employment in total labor in agriculture has risen, so that many more are earning cash incomes than before, the context is one of enforced female entry into the formal labor force. In these circumstances, the emergence of a secondary round of mechanization provoked by occasional labor bottlenecks is likely to be disastrous to poor rural women (Chatterji 1984).

In Africa, where food production is women's responsibility, agricultural investments have been made in nonfood crops as the profits from food production have declined relatively. In this case, women still do the work of food production but, over the long term, the rewards for their labor have fallen. In Africa, moreover, women's ability to produce food may in places be under challenge; population pressure is enhancing the scarcity value of land and women's traditional right of access to land may be jeopardized by the consolidation of formal land titles, which are usually given to male heads of families. Most recently, the collapse of many nonfood African export commodity prices has made food production more attractive in principle than formerly, though cheap food policies may mean that the relative prices facing agricultural producers still remain in favor of nonfood crops in some places. Innovative improvements in tropical plant varieties, which are said to be in progress, would increase food productivity and, hence, returns to women's labor, but they would also intensify these counteracting pressures.

In Latin America, tendencies of this kind are more advanced. While redistributing some of the land to agricultural wage laborers, the land reforms of the 1960s undercut the system of informal lease of vegetable plots to laboring families and so deprived women of the means to provide food for their own families' consumption. The recent commodity price falls have reduced many peasant households' cash income from sales of produce or labor on export crop production, while subsistence food production scarcely exists any longer to fall back on. Virtually removed from participating in agricultural production, many women have taken up informal industrial and services employment in the urban areas as a substitute, but this is a precarious source of income, vulnerable to fluctuations in the international economy. In this way, Latin American households have become split up in many cases; those that continue to pool resources have incomes drawn from more than one sector, and even rural households have become intricately connected with the urban economy and with the export international economy.

Industry

Industry has been the fastest growing of all sectors in developing countries over the postwar period, and the importance of women in the labor force in industry has been rising. Women now constitute 26.5 percent of the total industrial labor force in developing countries, compared with twenty-one percent twenty years ago. Countries that employ the highest proportion of women in their industrial labor forces have had the most successful growth records of all developing countries. Growth has created general employment opportunities from which women have benefited. However, women's greater participation has also played a significant *causal* role in industrialization, related to their lesser status and rewards in industrial production than men. In some regions, industrial development has added to women's income-earning opportunities to an extraordinary degree, but the terms on which they have found employment have been inferior. Therefore, despite the wage income, this new employment for women has not been unequivocally beneficial.

International markets and international institutions have been intimately involved in the expansion of industry in the developing countries. To take the institutions first, much of the industrial capacity in some regions in the earliest stages of industrialization, and also in the most recent period, has been built up under the aegis of TNCs. The expansion of production by TNCs' "sourcing" production abroad in cheap wage locations has reinforced developing countries' preexisting pattern of industrial product specialization in light industrial products, either traditional, such as garments and food processing, or modern, such as microelectronic components and appliances.

The market orientation of developing countries' industrial production has changed greatly over the past twenty-five years, in the direction of a dramatic shift toward international sales. Manufactured exports from developing countries grew at fifteen percent a year from 1963 to 1973 and eleven percent from 1973 to 1980, making this the fastest growing category of all goods traded internationally from whatever source. The dozen or so developing countries that account for the bulk of these exports now export on average almost sixty percent of their total manufacturing output, compared with only twelve percent in 1960. Transnational corporations are responsible for about one third of developing countries' manufactured exports.

There is a strong association between the growth of exports of manufactures and the growth of female industrial employment, which applies over both space and time. Just as the rate of growth of exports was significantly greater in the 1960s than the 1970s, the proportional increase in the numbers of women in the industrial labor force was faster in the earlier decade as well. By region, the absolute and relative growth of female industrial employment has been fastest in middle-income Asian countries, where most of the major developing country exporters are located, and lowest in Latin America, where the expansion of industry and exports has also been lowest. (Regional exceptions here, such as Brazil where export growth has been fairly strong, have also experienced geographically untypical rapid growth of female employment in industry.) In Latin America and elsewhere, under "import substituting industrialization" women are effectively kept out of employment in local, large-scale manufacturing industries. Their protected, uncompetitive nature means that these industries are able to offer high-paying jobs, which are mostly taken by males. Moreover, in some Latin American and Caribbean countries, there has been actual net displacement of women from the modern manufacturing sector in recent years.

Partly reflecting these patterns of growth, the relative importance of women in the industrial labor force now varies considerably by region, being highest in middle-income Asian and lowest in African and Latin American countries. In some of the most export-oriented industrializing developing countries, women constitute fifty percent of the manufacturing labor force, a significantly higher share than in any developed country.

Developing countries that sell manufactures abroad have in principle indefinitely large market prospects that have permitted many of them faster expansion of total industrial capacity than could be achieved by limiting sales to the domestic market. Part of the reason for the growth of female industrial employment in these countries thus lies in the strong general growth in labor demand generated by fast growth, which cannot be met in these places by male labor alone. But part of the explanation is more direct. The composition of manufactured exports is biased even more strongly toward labor-intensive light industrial goods than is the developing countries' total output of manufactures. The differentiation of the labor force by sex in terms of wages and other dimensions, such as docility, turnover, and promotional expectations, results in patterns of occupational segregation by sex that concentrate female labor in labor-intensive production in foreign and locally owned firms alike. Women constitute on average about three quarters of the labor force in garments and electronics, the most consistently "feminized" industries and the most important sources of exports.

Women's increased participation in modern industry in developing countries has conferred great benefits on women in terms of income and fuller participation in the formal economy. But these have been obtained at the cost of their subordination within this growing labor market, as in other spheres. The complexity of making an overall assessment is highlighted by controversy about conditions of employment in export processing zones, the duty-free enclaves where much export manufacturing, especially by transnational corporations, is carried out. Although wages are consistently lower for female workers *within* industries, in some new industries (and probably also within transnational corporations generally) female earnings are well above those available to women of equivalent qualifications anywhere else in the economy and also above anything available to *men* in many other parts of the industrial sector. Physical working conditions for women are poor in some respects, but it is difficult to say whether they are on average (or even in the worst cases) better or worse than those faced by male workers. However, women *are* more vulnerable to loss of employment and to the deterioration of working conditions when market conditions tighten. Employment in the electronics industry in particular has shown tremendous fluctuations over the past twelve years (albeit with a rising trend), which means that individual workers face extreme job insecurity. The implications of this are severe for women because they have far fewer other employment opportunities open to them than men do. Outside the electronics industry, women have suffered disproportionately from dismissal during cyclical downturns and during the world recessions, especially, but not only, in the export sector.

Industrial employment is not limited to factories. Much production takes place in the informal sector, where industrial outwork is subcontracted to factory employees in small workshops and to "homeworkers" (individual pieceworkers based in their homes). Both types of employment are considerably underreported in official statistics. Informal sector involvement is especially prevalent in labor-intensive production and by extension is also predominantly—perhaps almost exclusively in the case of homework—done by women. Informal sector industrial employment bears the same relationship to formal sector employment as female employment does to male within the formal sector: in both cases the former are less well paid in terms of both wages (often below subsistence level) and fringe benefits and far more insecure. For women ejected from the factory sector, the deterioration in employment conditions is marked. On the other hand, for women without any alternative prospects, the opportunity to do outwork is better than nothing, and the rewards are probably comparable with those of agriculture and the less rewarding parts of the service sector.

The growth of factory industry and employment in developing countries, with their involvement in international markets, has probably been associated with the expansion of extra, hidden employment for women in the informal sector because of the product specialization in labor-intensive goods. The level of informal sector activity is relatively high and seems to have been rising recently in Latin America. Recessionary pressures add to employers' incentives to use outworkers, and Latin American exporting firms, being relatively weak producers in international terms, may well have increased the ratio of outworkers to factory laborers. The prevalence in Latin America of informal sector industrial employment and women's strong representation in that sector offset the relatively low rate of participation by women in the formal factory sector in the region. This means that on the world scale, increases in industrial employment for women have not been so biased toward Asia as the official statistics suggest.

The most advanced of the industrializing developing countries (mostly in Asia) are beginning to enter high-technology manufacturing areas on the strength of their own financial, managerial, and technological capacity. These ''science-based'' industries provide more rewarding employment for workers who in most instances have to be highly skilled. Unless the prevailing pattern of occupational segregation by sex in industry is broken down, women are likely to be left out of this next phase of industrial development, disqualified by their lesser education and training, and the earnings differential by sex will start to widen. In some industrialized economies the tendency, by contrast, has been for a slight reduction over time in the gap between male and female earnings under the pressure of equal wage legislation and broader social change, including more education for women and their penetration of higher skill occupations.

Services

Services is the largest sector of activity in developing as well as developed countries. But as a sector it is heterogeneous in its range of activities, and even more subject than the industrial sector to official underrecording of employment, so that it is impossible to come to any definite quantitative conclusions about employment trends (for men or women) and the impact of international changes on this sector. Nevertheless, certain tendencies are likely, or at least can be inferred for particular individual service occupations, some of which are, undoubtedly, directly affected by international conditions.

The services sector includes formal and informal activities, highly skilled work and basic, unskilled work, including private and public sector employment and professional as well as personal services, ranging through administration, clerical, health, and education services, wholesale and retail trade, international banking and local money lending, tourism, domestic service, and prostitution, among other things. In many countries, these various services provide the bulk of national employment opportunities for women. This is particularly so in the developed industrial countries, where services are the main source of employment for the labor force as a whole, not just for women, and in Latin America, where fully sixty-three percent of the female labor force is occupied in this sector. In Africa and Asia, the services sector is both much smaller in the national economy and employs relatively fewer women. In Africa, however, retail sales, especially of food and food products in rural as well as urban areas, is a more or less female preserve, a spillover from women's important role in subsistence food production. In Latin America it can be said that, on the contrary, women's large presence in services is due to their *exclusion* from agriculture. Women migrate in greater numbers than men to the towns where, having little access to employment in manufacturing industry (at least in the factory sector), they have no alternative to doing whatever work is available in services. Domestic service is Latin American women's main source of employment, at low wages and often under poor conditions.

Some individual services are effectively secondary export activities, that is, they exist to faciliate the international exchange of the output of other economic activities. Financial services, commerce, and transportation may each in part serve international business. Growth of these services has been dependent on international competitiveness and market conditions in the same way as export of the tangible goods themselves. Although international financial and trade services proper are mostly located in the developed countries (with the exception of places like Hong Kong with an entrepôt history), the fastest growing exporting countries have experienced growth of their services sectors scarcely less fast than that of industry, which has probably been due in large part to a link with the manufacturing sector in general and thus to the growth of exporting in particular. Such services may be apparently local in scope, but in fact these services start exported products on the first stages of their journey. Tourism is a slightly different case, in that the scale of a country's tourist business is influenced by natural resource endowments and geographical location, on which is superimposed an erratic "business cycle" dependent on nothing so much as the fickle irrationalities of tourists' tastes and their perceptions of the political climate. Total worldwide tourist business, however, has grown very fast, even faster than total personal income, and developing countries have an important place in this expanding market.

Both tourism and general industry-related services will probably continue to be disproportionately important as sources of employment because productivity growth is slower than in industry. For the same reason, there may well be an increasing demand for *female* labor in these parts of the service sector, founded again (as in labor-intensive, relatively low-productivity manufacturing industry) on the cheapness of women's labor. Thus, tourism has so far been and is likely to continue to be a dynamic provider of jobs for women.

The rest of the services sector consists of a range of "nurturing" jobs in which women already predominate in many cases. Some are in the public sector, such as education, health, and administrative services; others are outside, serving private clients, often in the informal sector. The scale of the latter activities represents, among other things, a good index of the degree of personal income inequality. The personal services sector is relatively large in Latin America and small in middle-income Asian countries, which accords with other assessments of the degrees of income inequality in the two regions. The influence of international markets is felt in both cases, through different mechanisms.

The size and scope of public sector services, and the level of wages and of employment in this sector, is influenced by the level of the public sector deficit in relation to national income and exports. In heavily indebted countries, there is internal as well as external pressure (from creditors with policy leverage) on governments to reduce public expenditure. There is little information on the recent course of public sector service employment in such countries. This is especially unfortunate from the point of view of assessing overall trends in demand for female labor since the public sector is often a major employer of women. Given women's weak political position and the common patriarchal view that many welfare services merely supplement—or even supplant—the kind of services more properly provided by women within the household, the retrenchment of public welfare services, disproportionate job losses for women in the public sector, and increased demands on women themselves to provide welfare services for members of their family at home seem very likely.

On the other hand, it is very likely that through a process of widespread immigration and immiserization of the population under recessionary conditions, especially in heavily indebted economies, the numbers of people employed in private sector *personal* services, primarily domestic services, will increase, and these workers will mainly be women. Economic need drives more poor women to seek wage work, driving down the female wage rate in this catchall residual sector—by the same token, this increases the real income of the rich in terms of their ability to buy human labor sevices and their willingness to hire more domestic service. Both supply and demand factors serve to increase the level of employment. Again, the hypothesis entails an increase in female employment opportunities in this sector, but on worsened terms.

However, it should be stressed that this line of argument is purely hypothetical and speculative for both public and private sectors, in the absence of any evidence for the recent period. The speculations are worth putting forward, however, to dramatize the various possible implications of deterioration in the international environment for female employment in the sector, which in Latin America, if not any other continent of the developing world, is the largest employer of women at the present time.

Concluding Remarks

In short, the international context has affected the economic lives of women everywhere, perhaps even more than the lives of men. Changes in international markets have interacted with sexually divided patterns of activity to produce differential effects by sector and by region on men's and women's economic position. Since, even through periods of recession, international markets have grown faster than national output, sectors that have kept up or increased their share of world markets through exports have had higher rates of growth than those supplying only the local economy. In principle, therefore, where women have participated in production in successful export sectors, their employment prospects have improved. But the link is not automatic. It is mediated by the relative growth of labor productivity in such activities and dependent also on a generally buoyant national economic climate—failing which, women tend to get squeezed out of available jobs, even where there were previously sexually well-defined spheres of activity before.

In industry, women's jobs are concentrated, in both developed and developing countries, in poorly paid relatively labor-intensive branches. Labor-intensive products have formed the bulk of the developing countries' exports of manufactures, which have grown very fast; as a result, developing countries have increased their world market share. Employment opportunities for women in these industries have seriously declined in developed countries, but they have increased more than proportionally in the developing countries. No male labor–based industry has seen the geographical sources of world supply shift to this extent.

In agriculture, the effects of international changes on women have been more complex. The consequence of increased trade in this area has been that the prices of the agricultural products exported by the developed countries have fallen steadily in real terms. As importers and consumers, developing countries have benefited from falling prices. But only developing countries that managed to increase their yields of these products significantly have been able to maintain, let alone expand, their *earnings*. Elsewhere, with stagnant economies, returns to producers have fallen. It is mainly in Asia that productivity in grains has increased and mainly in Africa that it has remained static. In Asian countries, women's role in the agricultural production system has been affected by technological changes associated with productivity increases: not the technology of the high-yielding plant varieties themselves (which led at first to increased labor demands all round) but the subsequent mechanization introduced to cope with the greatly increased harvests. Mechanization tends to eliminate female labor tasks particularly, not only at harvest but throughout the year. In Africa, where women produce food crops, the failure to increase food productivity has steadily weakened women's income in this sector.

In services, no overall trends related to international factors are identifiable. The pattern of activity is complex and heterogeneous, and the analytical difficulties are compounded by enormous data weaknesses in this sector. This is particularly unfortunate in view of the importance of the service sector's considerable demand for female labor. In Latin America, where the services sector is disproportionately large and important as an employer of female labor, there are some indications that the scale of personal services, where women are the main providers of labor, may have been expanding relatively fast in the most recent period; however, the total picture is unclear. There is no doubt, however, that the conditions of work for women in this part of the services sector are very poor and probably deteriorating.

In all sectors—industry, agriculture, and services—therefore, some similarities are evident. Wherever women have gained or held onto employment, the work involved has carried a low reward relative to men's employment; international changes have done nothing to disturb and may even on balance have intensified this inferiority. Neither can international changes be said to have contributed in a major way to the worldwide increase in the labor force participation rate of women since the 1940s. In developed countries, where the increase was much more marked, the reasons why so many more women have sought paid work had little to do specifically with the international economy (except, importantly, where increased international activity led in general to economic growth); most new jobs for women have been in the locally driven services sector. In developing countries, rises in industrial employment attributable to international factors have only just outstripped loss of employment in agriculture.

But even though the overall rate of female income-earning economic activity has not changed significantly in developing countries in the postwar period, and even if, as suggested here, the conditions of women's work may have deteriorated relative to men's *within* each sector as a result of international economic pressures, one fundamentally beneficial change for women *can* be ascribed largely to international market changes. By leading to a relatively strong demand for female labor in industry, international factors have induced a significant shift in the distribution of female employment away from agriculture in developing countries. In 1980, 16.3 percent of women in the labor force in developing countries were in the industrial sector, compared with 12.5 percent ten years earlier. More than a quarter of the total industrial labor force in developing countries was made up of women in 1980, compared with one fifth twenty years earlier. Taking their lower overall rate of participation into account, by the end of the 1970s women were in fact better represented in industry in developing than in developed countries. The sectoral distribution of the male labor force in developing countries over this period changed in the same direction, of course, but the shift was less pronounced.

The implication of this change is very important. In all likelihood, among working women as a whole, there has been a definite improvement in women's economic status. This is because incomes are much higher in industry than in agriculture and higher also, though by a much smaller margin, than in the service sector. Women's earnings have therefore on average probably *increased* relative to men's over the past forty years. In this broad and basic sense, it is clear that the increased influence of international markets on economic activity in developing countries in the postwar period has *not,* so far as women are concerned, led to a repeat of the consequences of their first exposure to the monetization of markets in their local economies. The effect of the first monetization was to enhance the sexual division of labor by establishing the market place as the place for men while women, without monetary reward, provided household subsistence and maintenance. The wider scope of international exchanges has not reinforced that dichotomy.

The general thrust of policy recommendations for the benefit of women's employment prospects must be to enhance female participation further where possible, to protect such gains as have been made in the industrial sector in particular, and to improve the conditions of women's work where this does not militate against their chances of getting a job at all. What this implies for international and domestic policy measures is the subject of the next chapter.

9

Toward Innovative
Development Policies

The present international economic climate is fundamentally inimical to development. Employment prospects in general and particularly for the younger generation and for women have deteriorated drastically since 1980. Real interest rates are unprecedentedly high; the flow of external finance for development investment has almost dried up; and prices of commodities have either fluctuated widely or fallen in a sustained way. Instability and uncertainty are the order of the day for the majority of countries. With unemployment at record levels, industrialized countries have pursued nationalistic trade and monetary policies, which only worsen the situation. Heavily indebted developing countries and those still dependent on exports of primary commodities are struggling through times of domestic austerity, which are damaging to their productive capacity in the long run as well as immediately harmful to the standard of living of their populations.

In these circumstances, reassessment of national and international policies is imperative. Coordinated measures are required from the international community as a whole and from developing countries regionally and nationally. Only in this way will dynamism be restored to the world economy and conditions be made more favorable for national economic policies to create employment and cover the basic requirements of the population.

Progress in this direction is also vital if the slim advances made by

138

women in the past forty years are to be consolidated and carried further ahead. We have attempted to show the various influences on women—some positive, others damaging—specifically due to international factors. The balance of such influences will be more favorable against the background of an expansionary rather than stagnating international economy. The "Forward-Looking Strategies" adopted at the Nairobi Conference marking the end of the United Nations Decade for Women carried with them the unmistakable implication that the future position of women in the world economy rested on adjustments being introduced to the structure of international society and the world economy. Questions were raised with unprecedented frankness on the degree of willingness of states to forgo short-term self-interest in favor of international responsibility and solidarity; these precepts, enshrined in the United Nations Charter and in the Articles of Agreement adopted at Bretton Woods, have become sadly eroded as the current world economic recession has deepened.

There is great inequity in the allocation of world economic resources. Paradoxically, this is ground for optimism. It means not only that it is reasonable to hope for increases in worldwide production and economic and social progress if international economic relations can be improved, but it also suggests that measures directed to correct imbalances and specific areas of waste can be taken alongside international measures to boost levels of national economic activity. This will contribute to raising world demand and to reducing the beggar-my-neighbor impact of nationalistic policies widespread in the contemporary world.

Three areas of waste are particularly evident. The first is military spending; there is an urgent and pressing need for the worldwide burden of armaments expenditure to be curtailed and reduced. Such expenditures are inflationary; they drain scarce resources from public social and economic programs; and they divert investment from productive and peaceful pursuits. The stand of women's movements on this issue has had a major impact in turning the tide of world opinion against nuclear weaponry and the arms race, but it has had little if any effect so far on reducing the burden of arms expenditure. Second, concerted and harmonized international action is urgently needed to solve the chronic external debt burden of many developing countries. This is a common responsibility of the international community and one that cannot be resolved by approaching individual countries' difficulties piecemeal with short-term palliatives. Only with comprehensive reform and renegotiation of the international financial system can capital be diverted from destabilizing speculative activity and made available for investment purposes.

Third, women can be said to represent a major underutilized resource on the world scale. For a host of cultural, social, and economic reasons—which are self-perpetuating unless action is taken to break the cycle—restrictions are placed on the disposition and rewards of women's labor, depressing female productivity. By the same token, measures to improve women's economic position carry great potential for increasing total productivity; human labor in general, but especially female labor, remains for the most part underproductive, undereducated, and underpaid. Vigorous and sustained measures are needed to bring human resources, underused in this sense, fully into play in developed as well as developing countries to satisfy basic needs and observe human rights.

Improvement in women's economic position is directly relevant to the international dimension. In the first place, increases in women's participation in the modern sector are associated with greater competitiveness in international markets, as the experience of many developing countries has shown. Measures are needed to facilitate women's economic participation through education and social facilities. Relying on poverty and economic necessity to force more women into employment, at the cost of increases in their total work burden, will not be effective. Second, increased female participation in the labor force reduces income inequality between households; this helps to raise domestic saving and reduce reliance on external finance for development.

Policies to promote women's economic participation have to be comprehensive in scope and not limited to those sectors directly involved in international trade. Nevertheless, this study has some suggestions on the type of measures that would improve women's position in these activities.

A conclusion of this study has been that over the past twenty years or so, the expansion of the international economy has contributed to a rise in the level of gainful employment for women in developing countries and influenced the sectoral composition of women's jobs in favor of industry. Since industrial wages are generally higher than agricultural or service sector wages, increased international trade has helped to raise women's earnings relative to men's in some occupations. In that broad sense, international exchanges have been favorable to women's economic position. Women have gained most in terms of net employment creation in countries that have developed as successful exporters of manufactures. But it does not follow that "export promotion" of manufactured goods as normally narrowly defined is the answer, given the current state of the world economy. If, as at present, world trade remains almost stagnant, increased supplies will merely cut into the shares of preexisting exporters. Furthermore, in the two product areas in which developing country manufactures are concentrated, textiles and electronics, there are protectionist barriers to rich importing countries on the one hand and technological changes undermining developing countries' comparative advantage on the other. Both of these factors diminish the export prospects of developing countries.

We have shown that the international dimension is relevant to women across all sectors even in many activities apparently remote from international markets. What is required, accordingly, are wide-ranging policies to consolidate women's positions where advances have already been made, to reverse the harmful effects of international influences, and to attack conditions that perpetuate women's inferior position to men once they are in paid employment. Those predicted changes for the worse for women lie largely in the future. But there have been plenty of damaging effects already for women brought about by international factors. Prime among these is the economic devastation wrought in many developing countries outside East Asia, which have been caught in the debt trap and suffering falls in output and personal income in the worst general recession for fifty years. There are indications that women have been particularly hard hit by these events in both their capacities as paid workers and as managers of household resources. In the meanwhile, "adjustment programs" designed to lift countries out of economic crisis must take the gender dimension into account and trace their impact on women. Women's employment situation requires separate consideration because the stereotyped picture that women only provide extra income to families already supported by a male breadwinner is now far from universally valid. A high and probably increasing proportion—recently about one quarter—of all households in developing countries are headed by women. Millions of children are thus dependent on women's incomes for a better life. Furthermore, there is increasing evidence that in low-income families, children's health and nutrition benefit more from women's than from men's earnings.

It is particularly important to take steps to consolidate women's positions where international factors have already brought about some improvement. Present trends suggest that reversals may well otherwise set in, at least in industry and agriculture.

In the industrial sector, established exporters in all but the least developed countries are moving up the product scale to more capital- and technology-intensive products. Production of these goods provides employment only to highly skilled technical and managerial staff. Unless sex-biased educational and training programs are changed to give women the appropriate education for these positions, they will not qualify for these new jobs. The faster the rate of technological change, the more important this becomes. Women in developed as well as in developing countries will otherwise see their employment opportunities deteriorate relatively to mens'. Education and training for women to qualify them for nontraditional, technically advanced work is a priority in all countries.

In agriculture, new plant varieties have been introduced to great effect in certain parts of the developing world, notably in South and Southeast Asia. Greatly increased yields of rice and wheat have created demands for extra labor, both male and female, in these areas. Labor shortages have even appeared at peak times, provoking the introduction of labor-saving mechanized techniques. As with previous rounds of mechanization, this threatens to be applied particularly to female-specific tasks and thus to bring about massive displacement of women's labor. Efforts to reduce the sex bias in technological innovations are thus urgently necessary; women need training and information to help them make use of new techniques; and credit needs to be made available for agricultural tasks for women including small scale agro-industries, livestock raising, and other economic activities. In general, there is a need for compensating employment opportunities outside agriculture in rural industry and construction.

In agriculture, women in regions where high-yielding plant varieties have not been available have been severely damaged by international economic factors. Particularly in Africa, the interaction between the traditional division of labor by sex, whereby women are mostly responsible for growing food crops, and the price effects through international trade of greatly increased supplies of substitute grains has led to real falls in the value of women's output. Conversely, the fact of women's involvement in agricultural production in Africa to a greater extent than in other regions has led few resources to be invested in food crop production. Urgent steps need to be taken to reduce the difference in productivity between farmers growing new varieties and the rest. New varieties of rice and wheat suitable to different agronomic conditions need to be developed as well as new varieties of so-far unimproved family food crops such as cassava, yams, and sorghum.

Sub-Saharan Africa is increasingly recognized as a special case in view of the environmental degradation and, in some places, virtual collapse of the agricultural sector. A number of special multilateral funds have been set up for these countries. Arrangements to meet critical seasonal shortages of food crops should be linked to insurance measures for farmers, male and female, against the short-term effects of drought and the longer term effects of desertification. Proper recognition of women's actual role in agricultural production, particularly of food crops, is generally a precondition for progress in this area. Much of the problem in developing countries' agriculture can be traced to neglect of the gender dimension in investment and in technology programs. Even now, the link between channeling more resources to women and improving the productivity of agriculture has not yet been absorbed as a central principle. Securing women's access to land, capital, technology, and know-how, and supporting women's productive efforts with credit, are essential to any development program but especially vital in places where the viability of agriculture using low-productivity traditional methods of cultivation has been undermined by falling international prices.

Another drawback of employment for women related to international factors lies in the characteristics of women's work. While new employment opportunities have emerged for millions of women, the conditions of their work are often retrogressive. In the electronics industry, wages are not the lowest in the manufacturing sector and may be considerably higher than wages in the informal sector, but conditions continue to be difficult in terms of the types of jobs available and the duration of employment. Unless efforts are made to improve these aspects, trade-related employment will continue to provide dead-end low-skill jobs for women, replicating the worst features of the traditional segregation of occupation by sex.

The duration of employment for women in world market industries is often short. In the electronics industry, for example, marriage, let alone pregnancy, frequently disqualifies a woman worker. Employer practices thus reinforce the idea that factory wage employment, while presenting a lucrative period of a few years in which a young woman can contribute to her family's income, is a mere interlude in a life otherwise unchanged from the traditional cycle of childhood, marriage, and motherhood with dependence on a male breadwinner. Employment for a few years does little to challenge sex stereotypes and the wage differential by sex that ensues. This discriminatory practice should be ended, and women should be encouraged to continue paid work (not necessarily full time) irrespective of marriage and childbirth. In this way, attitudes toward paid employment for women will change, and women will develop a longer term view of progression in their work responsibilities and a tougher stance in wage negotiations. Employers should also be encouraged to implement existing legislation to provide on-site child care facilities. If there were a statutory obligation on *all* employers, whatever the sex of employees, then the conventional notion that child care arrangements were the woman's responsibility alone would be challenged. In the interim, in those countries where they do not yet exist, child care facilities should be provided in establishments with women workers.

Some of the employment for women in exporting industries has been directly or indirectly created by transnational corporations. Foreign corporations frequently locate their operations or give business to firms in developing countries where labor, in particular female labor, is cheap as well as generally educated and biddable. Nevertheless, the cost of improving female labor is a small element in total manufacturing costs. Pressure to raise wages and improve conditions for women workers will not deter transnational corporations, especially those with established operations, from offshore activity. Foreign firms may also be asked to set a leading example in other ways, increasing the numbers of women they train to higher level positions and employing many more women in senior posts.

The number of transnational corporations is increasing in the service sector, and pressure on them could begin to modify attitudes and employment practices in that segment of the labor market as well. Otherwise, the service sector is large, heterogeneous, and important to women as a source of employment and income. But both analysis and policy prescription are seriously hampered by lack of data in this area. Along with the need to investigate the relation between women's economic position and economic recession, the study of the service sector should be a high priority for research. In the meantime, governments should look to their own employment practices and ensure that employment for women is nondiscriminatory in the public sector as regards pay, promotions, and training and that layoffs in times of public expenditures cuts are not applied to women disproportionately.

In whatever sector women are employed, their position as workers is constrained by their domestic situation. Their child care and household-servicing responsibilities limit their mobility and flexibility in work and lead their employers to think they have little "commitment" to their jobs and are unsuitable for training and promotion. All policies and programs addressing women's employment have to straddle this "micro" dimension as well as the usual "macro" considerations of choices of technique, investment strategies, and so on. Measures aimed at improving women's position in the trade-related sector have therefore to fit into and be part of a program addressing women's position in the labor market as a whole. Such measures are unlikely to be effective unless the wider program is applied as well.

The "Forward-Looking Strategies" adopted by governments at Nairobi in 1985 constitute a package of measures of this kind. They are aimed mainly at governments and international donor agencies. These institutions are clearly important because of the public resources at their disposal and for their control of economic policy and legislation. Governments are also the only actors in a position to ensure enforcement of such regulations. Some of the recommendations relate to women as employees, others to self-employed women and women as operators of farms or small urban enterprises. In their totality, they would do much to remove employment discrimination against women and to increase the level of paid employment opportunities for them. On the labor supply side, improvements in the education and training of women are recommended, as are reentry programs for women, especially after childbearing. The incentives for women to seek work should be improved by changes in personal tax schedules; trade unions should promote the rights and rewards of working women; and maternity and social security schemes should be overhauled to encourage women to participate more fully in paid employment. On the labor demand side, flexible working hours for all men and women are recommended to accommodate the domestic constraints on women's time and also to enable men to share in household management. This would have the effect of making employers less biased against women on the grounds that—as is often true at present—they are unable to do overtime or commit themselves to night shift work.

Another recommendation is for credit to be made much more easily available to women producers in agriculture and in the service sector, where many women earn a meager livelihood and provide employment for other women. At present, women are commonly discriminated against by the conventional requirement for collateral set by lenders; hence, they are penalized by their restricted rights to owning property. But women's repayment record has been shown to be normally *better* than that of men in small-scale credit schemes where the collateral requirement is relaxed.

Measures to improve women's position are often seen as threatening to other interests. Even when this is not immediately the case, as when measures to improve women's productivity in self-employment benefit consumers as much as the woman operator herself, or when, in aggregate, increases in women's productivity and incomes are of general benefit, the fact remains that such improvements seem likely to increase women's bargaining position. There is a political dimension, therefore, to all of these recommendations. Women themselves have to act politically to advance their cause, using whatever form of organization is appropriate. Considerable emphasis was placed in the Nairobi "Forward-Looking Strategies" on the concept of self-reliance and on activities at the grass roots and community level, presupposing the mobilization of all local forces and resources as well as the involvement of international and national agencies. Sometimes labor unions will be the appropriate organizations, sometimes local-level women's organizations, and sometimes a national woman's movement or network. Sometimes international governmental groupings, such as the Organization for European Economic Co-operation and Development (OECD), the European Economic Community (EEC), and the Council for Mutual Economic Assistance (CMEA), will be most effective.

These latter may, with respect to employment in some sectors, be the *only* available organizations able to take action, because of conflicts of interest with women in developed countries. The internationalization of the textiles and elecronics industries, for instance, creates a situation where the interests of women workers in rich countries may be opposed to those of women workers (actual or potential) in developing countries, at least in the short run. But whether locally, nationally, or internationally, enhancement of political as well as economic bargaining power is the ultimate objective as well as the most effective instrument for reform. Not women alone, but men, children, and society as a whole stand to benefit from the change.

Annex

Excerpts on Women in Development: *International Development Strategy for the Third United Nations Development Decade*

1. Preamble

The development process must promote human dignity. The ultimate aim of development is the constant improvement of the well-being of the entire population on the basis of its full participation in the process of development and a fair distribution of the benefits therefrom. In this context, a substantial improvement in the status of women will take place during the Decade. In this perspective, economic growth, productive employment and social equity are fundamental and indivisible elements of development. (Paragraph 8)

2. Goals and Objectives

Full and effective participation by the entire population at all stages of the development process should be ensured.
In line with the Programme of Action adopted by the World Conference of the United Nations Decade for Women, women should play an active role in that process. Appropriate measures should be taken for

Exerpted from: *International Development Strategy for the Third United Nations Development Decade*, 1980, United Nations Department of Public Information, United Nations, New York.

profound social and economic changes and for the elimination of the structural imbalances which compound and perpetuate women's disadvantages. To this end, all countries will pursue the objective of securing women's equal participation both as agents and beneficiaries in all sectors and at all levels of the development process. This should include women's greater access to nutrition, health services, education and training, employment, and financial resources and their greater participation in the analysis, planning, decision-making, implementation and evaluation of development. Changes that will lead to the sharing of responsibilities by men and women in the family and in the management of the household should be encouraged. Institutional and administrative mechanisms to accomplish these objectives should be strengthened. (Paragraph 51)

3. Policy Measures

A. Industrialization

. . . Industrialization policies should have as one of their aims productive employment generation and the integration and equal participation of women in industrial development programs. (Paragraph 77)

B. Food and Agriculture

In the context of integrated rural development, Governments will encourage rural industrialization, the establishment and strengthening of agro-industrial complexes, the modernization of agriculture, better integration of women in all stages of the production process and the ensuring thereby of increased production of food and other agricultural products and employment for the rural population. (Paragraph 95)

C. Science and Technology for Development

All countries should seek to ensure that scientific and technological development will involve and benefit men and women equally and measures should be taken to facilitate equal access for men and women to scientific and technological training and to the respective professional careers. (Paragraph 122)

D. Social Development

. . . Countries will adopt effective measures to enhance the involvement of women in the development process. (Paragraph 163)

. . .

The important set of measures to improve the status of women contained in the World Plan of Action for the Implementation of the Objectives of the International Women's Year adopted at Mexico City in 1975, and the important agreed measures relating to the sectors of the International Development Strategy in the Programme of Action for the Second Half of the United Nations Decade for Women, adopted at Copenhagen in 1980, should be implemented. (Paragraph 168)

Bibliography

Ahooja-Patel, K. (1985). "The Place of Women in International Economic Relations," in Georgina Ashworth (ed.), *Women's Studies International* (special issue).

Anker, R. (1983). "Female Labour Force Participation in Developing Countries:A Critique of Current Definitions and Data Collection Methods," *International Labour Review* 122 (no. 6):709–723.

Armstrong, P. (1982). "If It's Only Women It Doesn't Matter So Much," in J. West (ed.), *Work, Women and Labour Market,* Routledge and Kegan Paul, London.

Batchelor, R.A., R.L. Major, and A.D. Morgan. (1980). *Industrialisation and the Basis for Trade* Cambridge University Press, Cambridge, England.

Beneria, L. (1981). "Conceptualizing the Labour Force: The Underestimation of Women's Activities," *Journal of Development Studies* 17 (no. 3):10–27.

Berry, A., and R.H. Sabot. (1978). "Labor Market Performance in Developing Countries: A Survey," *World Development* 6 (no. 11/12):1199–1242.

Boserup, E. (1970). *Women's Role in Economic Development,* Allen and Unwin, London.

———. (1980). In C. Presvelou and S. Spijkers-Zwart (eds.), *The Household, Women and Agricultural Development,* Miscellaneous Papers no. 17, Landbouwhogeschool, Wageningen, The Netherlands.

Bryceson, D. (1985). "Women and Technology in Developing Countries: Technological Change and Women's Capabilities and Bargaining Positions, INSTRAW, *Study on the Role of Women in International Economic Relations,* Santo Domingo.

CGIAR (Consultative Group on International Agricultural Research). (1985). *News* 5 (no. 2), World Bank, Washington, D.C.

Chatterji, R. (1984). "Marginalisation and the Induction of Women into Wage Labour: The Case of Indian Agriculture," ILO World Employment Programme, Research, *Working Paper WEP 10/WP. 32*, Geneva.

China. (1982). *Statistical Yearbook of China 1981* (English edition), compiled by the State Statistical Bureau, PRC, Economic Information Agency, Hong Kong.

Cockburn, C. (1981). "The Material of Male Power," *Feminist Review* no. 9:41–59.

Cohen, M. (1986). "The Influence of the Street Food Trade on Women and Children," in D.B. and E.F.P. Jelliffe (eds.), *Advances in International Maternal and Child Health*, Oxford University Press, New York and Oxford.

Eisold, E. (1984). "Young Women Workers in Export Industries. The Case of the Semi-Conductor Industry in South East Asia," ILO World Employment Programme, *Working Paper*, Geneva.

Elson, D., and R. Pearson. (1980). "The Latest Phase of the Internationalisation of Capital and its Implications for Women in the Third World," *Discussion Paper No. 150*, Institute of Development Studies, Sussex, England.

Flora, C.B. (1985). "Women in Agriculture," *Agriculture and Human Values* 2 (no. 1):5–12.

Frank, R. (1984). "Are Workers Paid their Marginal Products?" *American Economic Review* 74 (no. 4):549–571.

Gannicott, K. (1986). "Women, Wages and Discrimination: Some Evidence from Taiwan," *Economic Development and Cultural Change* 34:721–30.

Gidwani, S. (1985). "Impact of Monetary and Financial Policies Upon Women," INSTRAW, *Study on the Role of Women in International Economic Relations*, Santo Domingo.

Greenhill, C. (1984). "Manufactures and Semi-Manufactures: Twenty Years of Work in UNCTAD," *IDS Bulletin* 15 (no. 3), Institute of Development Studies, Sussex, England.

Griffith-Jones, S. (1983). "The Changing International Environment and its Impact on Developing Countries," *Discussion Paper No. 188*, Institute of Development Studies, Sussex, England.

Hakim, C. (1979). "Occupational Segregation: A Comparative Study of the Degree and Pattern of Differentiation between Men and Women's Work in Britain, the U.S. and Other Countries," *Research Paper No. 9*, Department of Employment, London.

Hopkins, M. (1983). "Employment Trends in Developing Countries, 1960–1980 and Beyond," *International Labour Review* 122 (no. 4):461–478.

Humphrey, J. (1984). "Growth of Female Employment in Brazilian Manufacturing Industry in 1970s," *Journal of Development Studies* 20:224–247.

Humphrey, J. (1985). "Gender, Pay and Skill: Manual Workers in Brazilian Industry," in H. Afshar (ed.), *Women, Work and Ideology in the Third World*, Tavistock Press, London.

IDS (Institute of Development Studies). (1981). "Women and the Informal

Sector," *IDS Bulletin* 12 (no. 3), Instutute of Development Studies, Sussex, England.

ILO (International Labour Organization). 1976. *Tripartite World Conference on Employment, Income Distribution and Social Progress, and the International Division of Labour.* Background papers: Vol. I, "Basic Needs and National Employment Strategies"; Vol. II, "International Strategies for Employment." Geneva.

————. (1980). Tripartite Committee on Textiles, *Report,* vols. 1 and 2, Geneva.

————. (1983 and 1984). *Yearbook of Labour Statistics 1983 and 1984*, Geneva.

ILO/INSTRAW. (1985). *Women in Economic Activity:A Global Statistical Survey, (1950–2000),* Geneva and Santo Domingo.

ILO/UNCTC. (1985). *Women Workers in Multilateral Enterprises in Developing Countries,* Geneva.

INSTRAW (International Research and Training Institute for the Advancement of Women). (1985). *The Role of Women in International Economic Relations: Summary of INSTRAW Series of Studies on the Role of Women in International Economic Relations,* Santo Domingo.

————. (1985). *Women and the International Drinking Water Supply and Sanitation Decade: Bibliography,* Santo Domingo.

Joekes, S.P. (1982a). *Female-led Industrialisation. Women's Jobs in Third World Export Manufacturing: The Case of the Clothing Industry in Morocco,* Research Report no. 15, Institute of Development Studies, Sussex, England.

————. (1982b). "The MFA and Outward Processing: Case of Morocco and Tunisia," in C. Stevens (ed.), *EEC and the Third World: A Survey 2,* Hodder and Stoughton, London.

————. (1985a). "Working for Lipstick? Male and Female Labour in Clothing Industry in Morocco," in H. Afshar (ed.), *Women, Work and Ideology in the Third World,* Tavistock Press, London.

————. (1985b). "Industrialisation, Trade and Female Employment in Developing Countries: Experiences of the 1970s and After," INSTRAW, *Study on the Role of Women in International Economic Relations,* Santo Domingo.

Knight, J., and R. Sabot. (1982). "Labor Market Discrimination in a Poor Urban Economy," *Journal of Development Studies* 19 (no. 1):67–87.

Krishnamurty, J. (1985). "Employment and Employment Policies in India" (mimeo), Delhi School of Economics, New Delhi.

Kuo, S. (n.d.). "Growth and Externalities of the Tertiary Industry in Taiwan 1952–1979," in K.T. Li and T.S. Yu (eds.), *Proceedings of Conference on Expenses and Lessons of Economic Development in Taiwan,* December 18–20, 1981, Institute of Economics, Academia Sinica, Taipei.

Lele, U. (1986). "Women and Structural Transformation," *Economic Development and Cultural Change* 34 (no. 2):195–222.

Lim, L. (1981). "Women's Work in Multinational Electronics Factories," in R. Dambert and M. Cain (eds.), *Women and Technological Change in Developing Countries,* Boulder Press, Colorado.

Lipton, M. (1983). "Demography and Poverty," *World Bank Staff Working Papers No. 623,* Washington, D.C.

———. (1985). "How Do Modern Varieties of Food Staples Affect the Poor?" (mimeo), Institute of Development Studies, Sussex, England.

Lloyd, C., and B. Niemi. (1979). *The Economics of Sex Differentials,* Columbia University Press, New York.

Malkiel, B., and J. Malkiel. (1973). "Male-Female Pay Differentials in Professional Employment," *American Economic Review* 63 (no. 4):693–705.

Marei, Wafaa. (1985). *The Importance of Research and Training to the Integration of Women in Development,* INSTRAW, Santo Domingo.

Molina, I., and R. Berio. (1986). "El Impacto de la Política Monetaria y Financiera en la Mujer Latinoamericana," INSTRAW, *Study on the Role of Women in International Economic Relations,* Santo Domingo.

Nogués, J., A. Olechowski, and L.A. Winters. (1985). "The Extent of Non-Tariff Barriers to Industrial Countries' Imports," World Bank, Development Research Department, Economics and Research Staff, *Discussion Paper No. DRD 115,* Washington, D.C.

North-South Institute. (1985). "Women and International Development Cooperation: Trade and Investment," INSTRAW, *Study on the Role of Women in International Economic Relations,* Santo Domingo.

OECD (Organization for Economic Cooperation and Development). (1976). *The 1974–1975 Recession and the Employment of Women,* Paris.

Page, S. (1981). "The Revival of Protectionism and its Consequences for Europe," *Journal of Common Market Studies* 20 (no. 1):17–40.

Pala Okeyo, A. (1985). "Toward Strategies for Strengthening the Position of Women in Food Production: An Overview and Proposals on Africa," INSTRAW, *Study on the Role of Women in International Economic Relations,* Santo Domingo.

Phillips, A., and B. Taylor. (1980). "Sex and Skill: Notes Towards a Feminist Economics," *Feminist Review* no. 6:79–88.

Portes, A., and L. Benton. (1984). "Industrial Development and Labor Absorption: A Reinterpretation," *Population and Development Review* 10 (no. 4):589–611.

Ryan, J.G., and R.D. Ghodake. (1984). "Labor Market Behaviour in Rural Villages in South India: Effects of Season, Sex and Socioeconomic Status," in H. Binswanger and M. Rosenzweign (eds.), *Contractual Arrangements, Employment and Wages in Rural Labor Markets in Asia,* Yale University Press, New Haven.

Sapir, A., and E. Lutz. (1981). "Trade in Services: Economic Determinants and Development-Related Issues," *World Bank Staff Working Paper No. 480,* Washington, D.C.

Schmitz, H. (1985). "Microelectronics: Implication for Employment, Outwork, Skills and Wages," *Discussion Paper No. 205,* Institute of Development Studies, Sussex, England.

Schuh, E. (1985). "Strategic Issues in International Agriculture" (mimeo), World Bank Agriculture and Rural Development Department, Washington, D.C.

Scott, B. (1985). "National Strategies," in B. Scott and G. Lodge (eds.), *US Competitiveness in the World Economy,* Harvard University Press, Cambridge.

Sen, A.K. (1985). "Women, Technology and Sexual Divisions," INSTRAW, *Study on the Role of Women in International Economic Relations,* Santo Domingo.

Sen, G., and C. Grown. (1985). *Development, Crisis and Alternative Visions: Third World Women's Perspective,* Development Alternatives with Women for a New Era (DAWN), New Delhi.

Sivard, R.L. (1985). *Women . . . a World Survey,* World Priorities, Washington, D.C.

Stern, B. (1985). "The Changing Role of Women in International Economic Relations," INSTRAW, *Study on the Role of Women in International Economic Relations,* Santo Domingo.

Taylor, L. (1982). "Back to Basics: Theory for the Rhetoric of the North-South Round," *World Development* 10 (no. 4):327–336.

Treiman, D., and E. Roos. (1983). "Sex and Earnings in Industrial Society: a Nine-Nation Comparison," *American Journal of Sociology* 89 (no. 3):612–651.

UNCTAD/INSTRAW. (1985). "Technology and Women's Status" (mimeo), INSTRAW, *Study on the Role of Women in International Economic Relations,* Geneva and Santo Domingo.

UNIDO. (1981). "Restructuring World Industry in a Period of Crisis—The Role of Innovation: An Analysis of Recent Developments in the Semi-Conductor Industry," *UNIDO Working Paper on Structural Changes,* UNIDO/IS 285, Vienna.

———. (1983). *Industry in a Changing World,* Vienna.

———. (1984). "The Role of Women in Industrial Development" (mimeo), Global and Conceptual Studies Branch, Geneva.

United Nations. (1976). *Report of Habitat: United Nations Conference on Human Settlements, Vancouver, 31 May–11 June 1976,* New York.

———. (1977). *Report of the United Nations Conference on Desertification, Nairobi, 1973,* New York.

———. (1979). *Report: World Conference on Agrarian Reform and Rural Development, Rome, 12–20 July 1979,* Food and Agriculture Organization of the United Nations, Rome.

———. (1980). *Report of the World Conference of the United Nations Decade for Women: Equality, Development and Peace, Copenhagen, 14–30 July 1980,* New York.

———. (1981a). *Report of the United Nations Conference on New and Renewable Sources of Energy, Nairobi, 10–21 August 1981,* New York.

———. (1981b). *Women and the Establishment of a New International Economic Order: A Selection of Recent Articles and Statements* (mimeo), New York.

———. (1985a). *Report of the World Conference to Review and Appraise the Achievements of the United Nations Decade for Women:Equality, Development and Peace, Nairobi 15–26 July 1985,* New York.

———. (1985b). *World Survey on the Role of Women in Development. Report of the Secretary-General,* New York.

———. (1985c). *Women and the International Drinking Water Supply and Sanitation Decade,* New York.

Urrutia, M. (1984). *Winners and Losers in Colombia's Economic Growth in the 1970s,* Oxford University Press for the World Bank, Washington, D.C.

Visaria, P. (1980). "Poverty and Living Standards in Asia: An Overview of the Main Results and Lessons of Selected Household Surveys," World Bank *Living Standards Measurement Study, Working Paper No. 2,* Washington, D.C.

World Bank. (1984a). *World Development Report 1984,* Washington D.C.

———. (1984b). *World Debt Tables,* Washington, D.C.

———. (1985). *World Development Report 1985,* Washington, D.C.

Index

157

INSTRAW's Series of Studies on the Role of Women in International Economic Relations

- *The Role of Women in International Economic Relations: Summary of INSTRAW Series of Studies on the Role of Women in International Economic Relations*
  Dominican Republic, 1985, 80 pp., Summary No. 1

- "The Changing Role of Women in International Economic Relations"
  Brigitte Stern
  Dominican Republic, 1985, 56 pp., Research Study No. 1-A

- "Women, Technology and Sexual Divisions"
  Amartya K. Sen at the request of UNCTAD and INSTRAW
  Geneva, 1985, 35 pp., Research Study No. 1-B

- "Women and Technology in Developing Countries: Technological Change and Women's Capabilities and Bargaining Positions"
  Deborah Bryceson at the request of UNCTAD and INSTRAW
  Dominican Republic, 1985, 44 pp., Research Study No. 1-C

- "Technology and Women's Status"
  UNCTAD/INSTRAW
  Geneva, 1985, 20 pp., Research Study No. 1-D

- "Impact of Monetary and Financial Policies Upon Women"
  Sushila Gidwani
  Dominican Republic, 1985, 44 pp., Research Study No. 1-F

- "Women and International Development Co-operation: Trade and Investment"
  North-South Institute
  Dominican Republic, 1985, 52 pp., Research Study No. 1-G

- "Toward Strategies for Strengthening the Position of Women in Food Production: An Overview and Proposals on Africa"
  Achola Pala Okeyo
  Dominican Republic, 1985, 36 pp., Research Study No. 1-H

- "Industrialisation, Trade and Female Employment in Developing Countries: Experiences of the 1970s and After"
  Susan Joekes
  Dominican Republic, 1985

- "El Impacto de la Política Monetaria y Financiera en la Mujer Latinoamericana"
  Iván Molina and Rina Berio; consultant, Ifigenia Martínez
  Dominican Republic, 1986

Available from the International Research and Training Institute for the Advancement of Women, Cesar Nicolas Penson 102-A, P.O. Box 21747, Santo Domingo, Dominican Republic.